THE SAINTS OF ANGLO-SAXON ENGLAND
Volume II

GLASTONBURY ICON OF THE MOTHER OF GOD

Courtesy of the Orthodox Church of St. Simeon and St. Anna, Devon

Volume II

THE SAINTS OF
ANGLO-SAXON ENGLAND
(9th to 11th Centuries)

by
Vladimir Moss

ST. NECTARIOS PRESS
SEATTLE, WASHINGTON
1993

THE SAINTS OF ANGLO-SAXON ENGLAND, Volume II

Published by
ST. NECTARIOS PRESS
10300 ASHWORTH AVENUE NORTH
SEATTLE, WASHINGTON 98133-9410

THE SAINTS OF ANGLO-SAXON ENGLAND series: ISBN 0-913026-33-6
Volume II: ISBN 0-913026-34-4

Library of Congress Number 92-82557

Printed in the United States of America

TABLE OF CONTENTS

LIST OF ILLUSTRATIONS

INTRODUCTION

FOR over 1000 years, from the coming of the first disciples of Christ to the Norman Conquest in 1066, there flourished in England that form of Christianity which today is found mainly in the countries of the Orthodox East: Greece, Eastern Europe and Russia...

This statement may surprise many people, especially Roman Catholics, who have been accustomed to believe that England was, until the Protestant Reformation, a Roman Catholic country. Was not England subject to the Pope for most of this period? Were not the Divine services in English churches conducted in Latin according to the Old Roman rite? Did not the English Christians accept many beliefs and traditions, such as the veneration of saints and relics, which are characteristic of Roman Catholic Christianity? Did not the schism between the Orthodox Church and Rome in 1054 pass almost unnoticed in England, and did not the English Church remain firmly in the Roman camp thereafter?

All this is true, but a closer examination of the facts will persuade us to give them a different significance. Thus the Popes to whom the English Church was formally subject were, in most cases, not papist in their faith, but Orthodox. St. Gregory the Great, for example, the apostle of the Anglo-Saxons, is accepted as a saint in the Orthodox Church; and it was he who proclaimed that any bishop who claimed universal jurisdiction over the whole Church — the Papist heresy in its earlier, and milder form — was "a forerunner of the Antichrist."[1] Again, the veneration of saints in the Anglo-Saxon

Church was authorized locally, without requiring the sanction of Rome; and it was only after the Norman Conquest that this thoroughly Orthodox practice — and the sanctity of many Anglo-Saxon saints — was questioned. And most significantly, although the 1054 schism itself was hardly noticed in England, the results of the schism, in the form of the Pope's sanctioning of the Norman invasion, his excommunication of the English King Harold and his followers, and the Normans' sacrilegious destruction of English churches and traditions was both noticed and fiercely resisted. Tragically, the resistance failed, the last "rebels" fled overseas (mainly to the centres of Orthodox Christendom in the East, Constantinople and Kiev) and England was incorporated by force into the new empire of the Roman papacy. But for generations after the Conquest, the popular conscience preserved the conviction that 1066 marked the end, not only of England's national independence, but also of her spiritual freedom, her adherence to the true, Orthodox faith of Christ.

Thus in the early twelfth century an anonymous English poet wrote: "The teachers are lost, and many of the people too"; and in the fourteenth Wiclif wrote that the true faith was preserved only in the East, among the Greeks. In the nineteenth century the historian Edward Augustus Freeman wrote: "The Norman Conquest is the great turning point in the history of the English nation... Its whole importance is not the importance which belongs to a beginning, but the importance which belongs to a turning point. So far from being the beginning of our national history, the Norman Conquest was the temporary overthrow of our national being."[2] And in our times R.H.C. Davis has written: "Apparently as the result of one days' fighting (14 October 1066), England received a new royal dynasty, a new aristocracy, a virtually new Church, a new art, a new architecture and a new language."[3]

In this series, a humble attempt is made to describe the old, true Church of England, that is, the Church which flourished before the Norman Conquest, through the lives of those of her saints who lived in the three hundred years from the first major incursion of the papacy into the affairs of the English Church, at the Council of Chelsea in 787, to the death of William the Conqueror in 1087.

This period has been chosen for a number of reasons. First, the saints' lives of this period represent an extraordinary spiritual treasure which is still largely unknown and untranslated. The lives of the great Celtic saints, such as David and Columba, Patrick, Samson and Kentigern, have been well served by translators. And the early Anglo-Saxon period has been immortalized both by the historical works of the Venerable Bede, which have all been translated, and by translations of Eddius Stephanus' life of St Wilfrid, Felix's life of St. Guthlac, and Willibald's life of St. Boniface. Gaps still exist; but by far the largest gap is constituted by the almost complete lack of translations of the very rich treasure of the ninth, tenth and early eleventh centuries.

Secondly, this period represents a certain historical unity in that it encompasses the fall of the seven ancient kingdoms of the Angles and Saxons under the pressure of the Viking invasions, the gradual emergence and consolidation of an All-English kingdom ruled (except for the brief interlude of the Danish monarchy) by the Wessex dynasty of King Alfred the Great and his descendants, and its collapse and integration into the empire of the medieval papacy as a result of the conquest carried out by William of Normandy and blessed by the future Pope Gregory VII (Hildebrand).

Thirdly, this period in English history coincides with the period of the decline and fall of the Roman papacy. Thus Rome's struggle with the Orthodox East began near the beginning of our period; and the final schism from Orthodoxy came in the middle of King Edward the Confessor's reign, with the Norman Conquest representing, as it were, the first crusade of the "Reformed Papacy" against the Orthodox Church. A study of this period is therefore important for an understanding of how not only England, but the whole of the West, fell away from Orthodoxy in the eleventh century.

The history of the people of God, whether in ancient Israel or Byzantium, England or Russia, is inseparably bound up with the acts of God Who is wondrous in and through His saints. Since God is their King, every important event in the Christian people's history reveals the Providence of God working through it for the enlightenment, chastizement, glorification or abandonment of His people. It is only when God has finally abandoned a nation that the important events in its history seem to be adequately described in purely political or economic terms, without reference to the workings of His grace; for, although God still works through nations that have forsaken Him, His workings are now more hidden in response to the hiddenness of the true faith in them. That is why the flow of miracles from the saints' relics gradually dries up, and why the bodies which have remained incorrupt for centuries often, although not always, return to the dust. It is not that God has ceased to work, or the saints to intercede: it is that no, or far fewer, signs are given to a sinful and adulterous generation....

Although this is not an academic-historical, but what is usually called a devotional work, every effort has been made to preserve historical accuracy. With regard to the thorny problem of the spelling of Anglo-Saxon names, the variety of translations used has necessitated some sacrifice in consistency. In general, however, the less authentic but (to a modern ear) more sonorous Latin transliterations have been used.

These books are dedicated to all the saints of England, in the faith and hope that those whose lives are translated herein will not be the last to flourish in our "land of the angels", as St. Gregory called it. For, as the Lord said through the Prophet Isaiah, "the isles will wait for Me...."(Is. 60.9)

INTRODUCTION TO VOLUME 2

ENGLAND, ROME AND CONSTANTINOPLE (2)

A great crisis in the history of the Church that was to take place in the pontificate of Nicolas I. For it was Nicolas, called "the Great" by papist historians but in truth one of the most power-hungry men ever to occupy the Roman See before the schism of 1054, who in 865 for the first time put forward the claim that the Pope had authority "over all the earth, that is, over every Church". This claim, which has no foundation in Holy Scripture or Tradition, was strenuously resisted by the Patriarch of Constantinople, as well as by some of the leading bishops of the West.

Thus the archbishops of Treves and Cologne replied to an unjust sentence by Nicolas in the following manner: "Without a council, without canonical inquiry, without accuser, without witnesses, without convicting us by arguments or authorities, without our consent, in the absence of the metropolitans and of our suffragan bishops, you have chosen to condemn us, of your own caprice, with tyrannical fury; but we do not accept your accursed sentence, so repugnant to a father's or a brother's love; we despise it as mere insulting language; we expel you yourself from our communion, since you commune with the excommunicate; we are satisfied with the communion of the whole Church and with the society of our brethren whom you despise and of whom you make yourself unworthy by your pride and arrogance. You condemn yourself when you condemn those who do not observe the apostolic precepts which you yourself the first violate, annulling as far as in you lies the Divine laws and the sacred canons, and not following in the footsteps of the Popes your predecessors...." [4]

Nicolas did not confine himself to unjustly deposing bishops within his own jurisdiction: he also deposed St. Photius the Great, Patriarch of Constantinople. Then, invoking an imperial tone, he demanded from the Emperor in Constantinople the return of his (Greek-speaking) territories in the south of Italy and Sicily for no other reason than that they had once, many centuries ago, come within the jurisdiction of the Roman Patriarchate when the Emperor resided at Rome: "Give us back the patrimony of Calabria and that of Sicily and all the property of our Church, whereof it held possession, and which it was accustomed to manage by its own attorneys; for it is unreasonable that an ecclesiastical possession, destined for the light and service of the Church of God, should be taken from us by an earthly power." Finally, and most importantly, he allowed the Filioque to be introduced into the Creed of the Latin missionaries in Bulgaria.

For this reason, a Council convened at Constantinople in 867 by St. Photius, and which included the archbishops of Treves, Cologne and Ravenna from the West, excommunicated and anathematized Nicolas. Two years later, however, a palace revolution enabled another, "anti-Photian" council to be convened, at which the Council of 867 was annulled. Romanists have often counted this anti-Photian council as the Eighth Ecumenical — not least, one suspects, because Pope Hadrian II demanded that all its members recognize him as "Sovereign Pontiff and Universal Pope".

But a much better claim to ecumenicity can be made for the Great Council convened at Constantinople in 879-80 by St. Photius, at which 400 eastern bishops were present together with the legates of Pope John VIII, and which annulled, under the legates' signatures, the acts of the anti-Photian council.

This Council also made two very important decisions. First, it decreed that there was no papal jurisdiction in the East, although the traditional primacy of the Pope was recognized. And secondly, it reaffirmed the original text of the Nicaean-Constantinopolitan Creed without the Filioque, and explicitly condemned all additions to it.[5]

It is a question whether the Filioque was in use in England at this time. We have already seen that Alcuin of York condemned it, which probably implies that the English Church, following Rome, did not use it in the eighth century. However, British clergy were in attendance at the Frankish council of Frankfurt in 794, at which the Filioque was adopted. And an Anglo-Saxon Homily on the Catholic Faith of uncertain date includes it. On the other hand, in the ninth century most professions of faith of newly elected English bishops neither affirmed nor denied the Filioque, stating simply: "I believe in God the Father, the Son and the Holy Spirit, [the Son] being born and having suffered for the salvation and redemption of the human race." It is only after the middle of the ninth century, and during the pontificate of Nicolas I, that the Filioque began to appear more often, as in the professions of the bishops of London, Hereford and Dunwich to Archbishop Ceolnoth of Canterbury. But in the same period, and in the same metropolitan province, the professions of the bishops of the royal see of Winchester, St. Swithun and Alfred, do not contain the interpolation.[6]

We may conclude, then, that the use of the Filioque was becoming more widespread in ninth-century England, but that some dioceses did not use it in their formal declarations of faith. The question now is: what difference did the Council of Constantinople's condemnation of the Filioque make? For one would naturally assume that, since the papal legates had signed the condemnation, and Pope John VIII had accepted the Council, he would be committed to seeing to the extirpation of the interpolation throughout his patriarchate.

He had a hard task ahead of him, however. As he wrote to St. Photius: "I think your wise Holiness knows how difficult it is to change immediately a custom which has been entrenched for so many years. Therefore we believe the best policy is not to force anyone to abandon that addition to the Creed. But rather we must act with wisdom and moderation, urging them little by little to give up that blasphemy. Therefore, those who claim that we share this opinion are not correct. Those, however, who claim that there are those among us who dare to recite the Creed in this way are correct. Your Holiness must not be scandalized because of this nor withdraw from the sound part of the body of our Church. Rather, you should aid us energetically with gentleness and wisdom in attempting to convert those who have departed from the truth...." [7]

St. Photius seems to have accepted this, and remained in communion with Rome for the rest of his life, referring to the Pope as "My John". But in 903 St. Nicolas the Mystic, Patriarch of Constantinople, broke communion with Pope Christopher because the latter introduced the Filioque into the Creed of the Roman Church for the first time. This may have happened again in 1009, for in that year the Pope's name was removed from the diptychs of the Church of Constantinople, although public communion was not broken; and in 1014 the Filioque was certainly used at the coronation of the German Emperor Henry I in Rome.

A similar pattern may be observed with regard to the question of papal supremacy — that is, a more or less complete suppression of the error in the tenth century, and its resurgence in the eleventh. Several factors contributed to this. One, paradoxically, was the moral degradation of the papacy during this period, which lowered its authority in the eyes of the people. Thus late in the ninth century we see the extraordinary spectacle of Pope Stephen VI exhuming the remains of his predecessor Formosus, solemnly anathematizing the rotting corpse, and then throwing it into the Tiber! Again, much of the tenth century papacy was controlled by the "pornocracy" of the prostitute Theodora and her daughters Marozia and Theodora, who disposed of the senior see of Christendom in favour of their sons and lovers. One of the Popes of this period was only twelve years old! It was scandals such as these, together with the approach of the millenium, which prompted a Council of French and English bishops meeting in Rouen in 991 to speculate whether they were witnessing the coming of the Antichrist.

A second factor was the political chaos produced in the West by the repeated invasions of Vikings from the North, Magyars from the East and Saracens from the South. In such circumstances, Christians battling for survival looked, not to an impotent Pope in faraway Rome, but to local leaders with the skill and determination to protect them from their enemies. Thus the Christian leadership of the West fell, of necessity, to such rulers as Alfred the Great in England and Otto the Great in Germany.

A third factor was the control exercised by the German "Holy Roman Emperor" over the papal see. We have already seen the beginnings of this control under Charlemagne. But by the time of Otto the Great, the control was much greater. The elected Pope had to take an oath to the imperial legates who were thereby in a position to veto the suitability of the papal candidates. And so, being a vassal himself, the Pope was in no position to claim universal supremacy! [8]

Map of Dioceses, c. 1000

ST. DUNSTAN

Icon courtesy of the owner

ST. DUNSTAN
(MAY 19)

OUR holy father Dunstan was born in the village of Baltonsborough, near Glastonbury, in about the year 909. His parents were of noble stock, and were called Herstan and Cynedritha. When the saint was still in his mother's womb, she went to church on the Feast of the Meeting of the Lord — Candlemas, as it is known in the West. According to the custom, everyone was holding lighted candles in their hands. Suddenly all the candles went out. Equally suddenly, Cynedritha's candle was rekindled; the amazed congregation then rekindled their own from hers. This was taken as a sign that the child she was carrying would be a great light in the Church, from whom many others would draw enlightenment and inspiration.

The saint knew Glastonbury from his earliest years. According to an ancient tradition then current, the first Christians who came to England found at Glastonbury "an ancient church not built by human hands and prepared by God for the salvation of men, which the Lord by many miracles showed to have been dedicated to Himself and the Most Holy Mother of God Mary."[9] Once the young Dunstan was taken there on a pilgrimage by his father. During the night an old man dressed in a shining white garment appeared to him in a vision, and led him through all the rooms of the holy church. He also showed him the monastery buildings which were to be built by him during his abbacy in the very order in which they were later constructed.

On seeing their son's promise, Herstan and Cynedritha sent him to Glastonbury to be educated. Like a bee, he darted through many fields of religious literature. He also learned from the Irish pilgrims who came to venerate the tomb of St. Patrick. [10]

Once he fell ill and was on the point of death. In the middle of the night, however, he received a sudden access of strength, and, springing up immediately, went with God's guidance towards the monastery. Some dogs rushed at him, barking furiously; but he repulsed them with a thin twig and carried on. Having arrived at the church, he climbed onto the roof by a route that the workmen used, and, descending down the other side, came to a little chamber, where he innocently fell asleep. There he was found the next morning, to the amazement of everyone. For he had been at the point of death, as his nurse witnessed, and the chamber was very difficult to get to. The nurse was especially amazed, and went up onto the roof to take a look round.

Besides his religious activities, Dunstan cultivated the arts of metalworking, painting and harp-playing. One day, he was invited to the house of a certain noblewoman named Ethelwynn. She had asked him to design a stole to be used in the Divine services which she would then adorn with gold and silver and precious stones. Dunstan came, bringing his harp with him. Then, as they were returning to work after supper, the harp, which was hanging on the wall far from the reach of any visible hand, spontaneously began to play the melody of the hymn: "Let the souls of the saints who have followed in the footsteps of Christ rejoice in the heavens. Since they shed their blood for His love, they will reign with Christ forever!" Everyone was amazed at the miracle, wondering what it could mean.

In 923, Archbishop Plegmund of Canterbury reposed in the Lord, and was succeeded by Dunstan's uncle, Athelm, the bishop of Wells. Athelm invited the saint to stay with him at Canterbury in the archbishop's house, and Dunstan accepted. Archbishop Athelm foresaw the future greatness of his nephew and introduced him to King Athelstan, who showed him great favour.

But then a temptation was allowed to try him. Certain companions and relatives of his at the court became jealous of Dunstan's success and accused him to the king of practising black magic. The soldier of Christ did not falter, but remembered the words of David: "Unjust witnesses are risen up against me, and injustice hath lied to itself." He placed before his spiritual eyes the promise of Christ: "Blessed are ye when men shall revile you and persecute you and say all manner of evil against you falsely for My sake. Rejoice and be exceedingly glad; for great is your reward in heaven." And so, comforted by these words, he "became as a deaf man in whose mouth are no reproofs"; for when the dogs barked at him he hardly ever opened his mouth. But their madness grew more frenzied, and, binding him like a sheep by the arms and legs, they threw him into a muddy pool and trampled on him. He got up and set off for a friend's house which was about a mile away. But then the friend's dogs ran keenly up to him, and, thinking him to be more a monster than a man, started barking at him savagely. However, they soon recognized his soothing voice and calmed down. Sighing deeply, the servant of God reflected how the irrational nature of animals showed him more kindness than the animal ferocity of his kinsmen.

Shortly after this, the saint went to stay with another relative of his, St. Alphege "the Bald", bishop of Winchester. Once the holy bishop was going with Dunstan to the dedication of a church at the west gate of the city. After the festivities, when they were returning past the church of St. Gregory, the bishop called a halt for Compline. As they were putting their heads together for the absolution, a stone suddenly fell out of the empty sky and passed between them, injuring no one but grazing their heads. Where could this come from, people reflected, if not from the evil one?

Alphege several times asked Dunstan to become a monk. But he refused, pleading that he wanted to marry. Then the bishop prayed to the Lord that the young man would pay heed to his warnings. Immediately Dunstan was seized by an intolerable pain in his bladder which passed to his whole body. Thinking that he had elephantiasis and that he was on the point of death, in great anguish he sent for the holy bishop whom he had just spurned. When the bishop arrived, he announced to him his intention of following his salutory advice. Chastened, and now recovered from his illness, Dunstan received the monastic tonsure.

St. Alphege also ordained him to the priesthood, and then sent him back to Glastonbury. There he built for himself a very narrow cell in which to fast and pray. He also occupied himself in making church bells and other ecclesiastical ornaments.

Now there died a close friend of the saint's, a deacon by the name of Wulfred. Not long after his death, Wulfred appeared to Dunstan and revealed to him many heavenly mysteries, as well as the whole course of his future life. When Dunstan asked for a sign whereby he could be assured of the truth of these revelations, Wulfred led him to the cemetery, and, pointing to an unused plot, said: "You will know that what I say is true from the fact that in three days' time a priest will be buried here, although he has not yet fallen ill." On awaking, Dunstan related the prophecy to some others; and as they were coming back from the cemetery the chaplain of a certain very religious noblewoman came up and asked for that plot for his burial. Shortly after, he sickened and died; and within three days he had been buried in that very spot.

Now Ethelfleda was a very rich woman of royal birth and strictly religious upbringing who, on the death of her husband, wished to lead a widow's life in accordance with her strength. She bought a small house near the church so as to be able to serve the Lord day and night. Dunstan loved her very much; and she diligently supported him for Christ's, as well as for kinship's sake.

Among other good works, she was much given to hospitality; and on one occasion she prepared a meal for King Athelstan, who was coming to Glastonbury to pray. The day before his visit, the king's stewards came to see that everything was suitably prepared, and remarked that there was not enough mead. She replied: "My mistress, the Most Holy Mother of God, will not let me go short, either in mead or in anything else pertaining to the royal dignity." After saying this, she entered the Old Church, and, prostrating herself, prayed to the King of all that He would grant her an abundance of provisions for the service of the king.

The king duly arrived with a large company in attendance. After the Divine Liturgy, he joyfully came to his invited seat. The supply of mead was exhausted at the first toast, but God abundantly made up the deficiency so that nothing was lacking for the whole day. However, when the king's servants told him of the miracle, he abruptly stopped and said to his men: "We have sinned by over-burdening this handmaid of God with our unnecessarily large numbers." And getting to his feet, he bade farewell to her and continued on his way.

Ruins of St. Mary's Chapel, Glastonbury

Now Ethelfleda fell seriously ill, and the saint prepared her for her end, looking after her as if she were his own mother. Because of this, he was late for

Vespers one day, and at dusk came back to the church to celebrate the delayed service. As he was standing outside the church chanting psalms with the brethren, he saw coming from the direction of the setting sun a white dove of extraordinary beauty with wing-tips sparkling like fire that entered the house of Ethelfleda.

After the service, the saint went back to the house. Standing by the curtain at the entrance to her bedroom, he could hear her having a serious conversation with what seemed to be an intimate friend; and, wondering who it was, he went and asked her maid-servants who were standing nearby. They replied that they did not know. "Before you came," they said, "the chamber was filled with a reddish light of extraordinary splendour. That has stopped, but she, as you can hear, has not ceased from carrying on a conversation with her interlocuter." Dunstan sat down until she had finished her conversation. Then, drawing back the curtain, he entered her room and asked her with whom she had been speaking. "You yourself saw him coming before you came here," she said, "and do you ask me now with whom I was speaking? For he who spoke with me is the same person who appeared to you as you were chanting psalms outside the church. And he told me in private everything concerning my departure from this life. But there is no need for you and your friends to weep for me — God will graciously visit me at my death and allow me to enter into the joys of Paradise. However, I want you to do this for me as I were your only friend: hasten early in the morning, prepare a funeral vestment for me to wear, make ready a bath, and after my bath celebrate the Divine Liturgy, communicating me in the Holy Body and Blood of our Lord Jesus Christ. At that moment, with God leading me, I shall go the way of all the earth." Dunstan promptly obeyed the blessed lady's commands to the last detail. And after partaking of the Holy Mysteries, just as the Liturgy was coming to an end, she gave up her soul into the hands of her Creator.

In 939, King Athelstan died, and was succeeded on the throne by King Edmund. Dunstan became one of his counsellors, for his court at Cheddar was not far from Glastonbury. As in Athelstan's reign, this provoked the envy of some of the courtiers, who slandered the saint to the king and procured his banishment. Dunstan then asked the help of some foreign envoys who were then at the court, and they, taking pity on him, promised him their hospitality and everything he might need if he accompanied them back to their kingdom.

The next day the king rode out hunting with his men. As they came to the forest, they dispersed in friendly competition along different paths. However, the baying of the dogs and the calling of the horns enabled many of the stags to make a quick escape; and only the king, with one pack of dogs, found himself on a stag's track. In his flight the exhausted animal came to a very deep gorge into which he suddenly hurled himself, followed by the dogs. The king, following close behind, was accelerating when he saw the gorge. Desperately, he tried to hold back his horse, but without success. With all hope for his life gone, he commended his soul into the hands of God, saying within himself: "I thank Thee, O God Most High, that as far as I can remember, I have not harmed anyone at this time, except only Dunstan, and I shall be reconciled with him promptly if my life is saved." When he had said this, his horse came to a standstill on the very edge of the abyss.

Praising and giving thanks to God, the king realized that he had come so near to being killed in order that Dunstan might be vindicated; and on his return he ordered him to be brought before him without delay. When Dunstan came in, he said: "Hurry up, get a horse, and come with me and my soldiers." And, mounting their horses, they immediately took the road to Glastonbury. On arrival, they went into the church to pray; and after praying and wiping the tears from his eyes, the king again called the servant of God to him. Taking him by the hand, he kissed it and led him to the priest's chair. Having seated him in it, he said: "Be the powerful incumbent of this seat and the most faithful abbot of this church. And whatever you need, whether for the Divine services or for the sacred Rule, I shall devoutly supply from my royal bounty."

ABBOT OF GLASTONBURY

Dunstan was placed in charge of Glastonbury in 943, and immediately instituted the strict application of St. Benedict's Rule for the monks, thus giving a major further impetus to monasticism in England after the devastation of the Viking wars. He also began to build many buildings for the monastery in accordance with his childhood vision. One day, a great beam was being raised to the roof of the church, and was about to touch it when it began to tilt downwards and fall, threatening the lives of many people below. A cry went up from the ground, which drew the saint's eyes to the scene. With his right hand he made the sign of the Cross, and lo! by the invisible power of God the beam was restored to its place.

Enraged by these miracles, which were drawing the souls of their beholders closer to the Lord, Satan tempted the saint by appearing to him in many fearful guises. One night, as he was keeping vigil at the altar of St. George and resting little, the devil came up behind him in the form of a bear threatening to devour him. At first the man of God tried to beat him with a staff which he always carried with him; but to no avail. Then he resorted to the stronger spiritual weapon of psalmody: "Let God arise, and let His enemies be scattered, and let them that hate Him flee from before His face." The deceiver fled in confusion.

Through another vision of evil spirits, the saint prophesied the death of King Edmund. For as he was travelling in the king's escort, he suddenly saw a black form running among the king's trumpeters. After gazing at it for a long time in amazement, he turned to his neighbour, 'Half-King' Athelstan, the alderman of East Anglia, and said: "Beloved, do you see what I see?" "Nothing out of the ordinary," he replied. "Sign your eyes with the sign of the Holy Cross, and then see if you can see what I see," said the holy man. When he did this, Athelstan also saw the evil spirit. When they made the sign of the Cross again, the enemy disappeared.

As they continued on their way, Athelstan asked the saint to what extent this vision of theirs was related to a dream he had had, in which he had seen the king fall asleep while feasting amongst his nobles, whereupon almost all the chief men and counsellors had turned into sheep and goats. Dunstan immediately replied: "The king's sleep means his death; but the changing of the chief men and counsellors into mute and irrational beasts refers to the future, when almost all the chief men and rulers will of their own accord deviate from the way of truth."

As they came to the king's quarters, they were still discussing these matters. And at dusk on the same day Dunstan again saw the evil spirit wandering among the servants at the king's banquet. Then, on the very day on which the king was killed, May 26, 946, he saw it for the third time as the king was returning from the Divine Liturgy to the banquet-hall. During the feast, the king saw a man named Liofa, whom he had banished from the kingdom six years before, sitting at a table next to an alderman. He got up and tried to drive the outlaw from the hall, but was stabbed by him and died. The king's body was taken to Glastonbury, where St. Dunstan performed the funeral service.

Edmund was succeeded by his brother Edred, who loved Dunstan no less than his predecessors, loading him with honours and submitting to his wise counsel.

In 953, Bishop Ethelgar of Crediton, in Devon, died; whereupon King Edred tried to persuade the saint to accept the vacant see. But he refused, not wishing to desert the king, whom he loved, for the sake of the episcopate. The king then asked his mother, St. Elgiva, to intercede. So she invited him to a royal banquet and again put forward the same proposal. But he replied: "I ask you, lady, not to ask me this again; for I tell you truly: I must not be made a bishop during the lifetime of your son the king."

The Lord, however, was not pleased by the saint's refusal, as was revealed to him in a vision that night. For he saw himself returning from a pilgrimage to the apostles' tombs in Rome and was coming near the Mons Gaudium. Then St. Peter and his fellow apostles Paul and Andrew approached him. Each held in his hand a sword, which they offered him. On Peter's sword were inscribed the words: "In the beginning was the Word, and the Word was with God, and the Word was God." Then Andrew sang sweetly from the Gospel:

"Take My yoke upon you, for I am meek and lowly of heart, and ye shall find rest unto your souls." Peter then raised a staff which he held in his hand and struck Dunstan lightly on the palm, saying: "Take this as a warning not to refuse the yoke of the Lord in future." Waking up, the saint asked a monk who was sleeping in the same room as he who it was that had struck him. He said that he did not know. Dunstan thought for a while, and then said: "Now I know, my son, now I know by whom I have been struck." In the morning he recounted his vision to the king, who said: "Since the swords you took up with the apostles' blessing are the weapons of the Holy Spirit, you can be quite certain that through the sword given you by the blessed Peter and inscribed with the word of God, you are to receive the archbishopric from heaven." As for the other swords, that given by St. Paul may have signified the see of London, whose cathedral church was dedicated to the apostle and which Dunstan held for a short period before he became archbishop. And that of St. Andrew may have signified the see of Rochester, whose church was dedicated to the First-called and which Dunstan was called upon to defend in his later years.

King Edred had been chronically sick throughout his reign, and now he came to die. Feeling his end draw near, he sent a messenger to Dunstan to bring his treasures from Glastonbury, where the saint had been looking after them, to Frome, where the king lay. As Dunstan was riding from Frome, on St. Clement's day, 955, he suddenly heard a voice from heaven: "King Edred now rests in peace." At the sound of the voice, his horse, unable to bear the angelic power, fell dead to the ground, astonishing the saint's companions. When he had explained to them the voice and its meaning, and as they were blessing God and commending the soul of the dead man into the hands of God, messengers came up and confirmed the truth of the voice. And so the walls of the palace were resounding to cries of lamentation as the saint entered. He found the royal corpse abandoned; and so, faithful in death as in life, he performed the funeral service and buried the king in the Old Minster, Winchester. [11]

The death of King Edred marked the end of Dunstan's peaceful tenure of the Glastonbury abbacy. For he was succeeded by Edwig, the son of King Edmund — a rash youth under the influence of a mother and daughter, both named Elgiva, who wanted him to choose one of them to be his wife. He acted wantonly with them in public, which caused scandal among the people.

The time came for the anointing and consecration of the king after his election by the people. The ceremony was duly performed, but after it the king had no time to attend the banquet with his nobles and bishops, but immediately ran after the loose women. When Archbishop Oda saw that the king's willfulness, especially on the day of his coronation, displeased all the councillors sitting around, he said to his fellow-bishops and the other leading men: "Let some of you, pray, go and fetch the king, so that he may, as is fitting, be a pleasant companion to his followers at the royal banquet." But one by one, fearing to incur the king's wrath or the women's complaint, they began to demur. Finally they chose from among them two whom they knew to be most firm in spirit — Abbot Dunstan and Bishop Cynesige, a kinsman of Dunstan's, to go in obedience to the command of all and bring back the king, whether he wished it or not. Entering the king's chamber in accordance with their superiors' command, Dunstan and Cynesige found the king's crown, which was bound with gold, silver and precious stones, and shone with a many-coloured light, carelessly thrown on the floor far away from his head, and himself wallowing between the two women as if he were in a sty. They said: "Our nobles have sent us to you to ask you to come as quickly as possible to your proper seat, and not to scorn to be present at the joyful banquet of your chief men." But when he did not wish to rise, Dunstan, after first rebuking the folly of the women, drew him by his hand from his licentious reclining with them, replaced the crown on his head, and brought him with him to the royal assembly by force.

Like Jezebel of old, the elder Elgiva now conceived a violent hatred of Dunstan and obtained the consent of the king to deprive him of all his honours and possessions, and to expel him from the kingdom. Dunstan's friends and supporters were also persecuted. Elgiva even sent agents to kill Dunstan before he could leave the country. But he eluded her grasp, and made a speedy passage to the continent. There he was kindly received by Arnulf, Count of Flanders.

There the saint did not cease to weep and groan day and night, thinking of his country and the spiritual condition of his monastery.

One night, he dreamed that he was with a group of the brethren as they were coming to the end of the Vespers psalms. After the canticle, "My soul doth magnify the Lord," they began to sing the antiphon from Job: "Why have ye disparaged his truthful words, and composed speeches to reprove him, and..." At this point the chant stopped and they all fell silent; nor was he able to persuade them to complete either the words or the melody. Several times they went back to the same point in the chant, never did they say the last words. And he, rebuking them in the same vision, said: "Why do you not want to end the antiphon with the words:

'what ye have had in mind ye discharge'?" Then came the Divine reply: "Because, I say, they will never discharge what they are striving for in their minds — to tear you away from the government of this monastery." Waking up, the saint gave thanks to God the Most High, his Comforter. And indeed, some of the people in the vision turned out later to have been plotting against him secretly.

King Edwig married the younger Elgiva, although the union was within the forbidden degrees of kinship. As a result, the northern kingdom of Mercia and Northumbria rebelled against him, and chose his brother Edgar as their king; and in the next year Archbishop Oda dissolved his marriage. When Elgiva tried to rejoin him, she was caught by men of the northern kingdom, who severed the muscles and sinews of her lower limbs; whereupon she died in agony a few days later. Finally Edwig died, and when Edgar reunited the kingdom under his sole rule, he recalled Dunstan from exile...

ARCHBISHOP OF CANTERBURY

In the year 958 King Edgar "the Peaceable" ascended the throne; and in the same year St. Dunstan was made bishop, first, of Worcester, and then, in 959, of London, before being elected archbishop of Canterbury in 960. The truly "symphonic" cooperation of King Edgar and Archbishop Dunstan marked the beginning of the golden age in the history of the Anglo-Saxon Church, which age had been prophesied by a heavenly voice which St. Dunstan had heard in 943, at the birth of Edgar: "Peace to England as long as this child reigns, and our Dunstan survives." "The succession of events," writes William of Malmesbury, "was in unison with the heavenly oracle; to such an extent did ecclesiastical glory flourish and martial clamour decay while he was alive."[12]

ROMSEY ABBEY
King Edward confirmed the privileges of Romsey to nuns in 966.

However, the early part of Edgar's reign was marred by his attempts to seduce two nuns of Wilton, St. Wulfhilda and Wulfrida, by the second of whom he had a daughter, St. Edith. For this he was placed on a penance by St. Dunstan, and was not allowed to wear his crown from his sixteenth to his thirtieth year. He accepted this penance humbly, and it is probably for this reason that his coronation did not take place until the year 973, in a ceremony in Bath Abbey which became the model for all future English coronations. [13]

After Dunstan had been elected archbishop, he set off, like all English archbishops-elect, for Rome, to receive the pallium from the Pope. On the road he gave away all his provisions to the poor, which greatly irritated his servant. So when he asked one day: "What do you have to sustain us tonight?", the servant replied: "Absolutely nothing; for you have taken no care to anything, you gave it away, either to our own men or to strangers." Then the bishop said: "I ask you not to be too worried by this; for Christ our Lord is bountiful to all those who believe in Him." But the steward replied again: "Now you will see what your Christ will give you tonight — you who have squandered everything." And he continued scoffing as the saint went in search of a place to serve Vespers. His scoffing soon ceased, however, when the bishop was met by messengers of an abbot who had been waiting for him for three days, and who now most charitably supplied the needs of the saint and his men for many days ahead.

On returning from Rome, Dunstan immediately set about spreading the monastic reforms which he had initiated at Glastonbury; and he found the king a willing helper in this holy task. Already, as bishop of London, he had founded a small monastery of twelve monks at Westminster with Saint Wulsin as abbot. Now he appointed his disciples Saints Oswald and Ethelwold, both zealous monks, to the sees of Worcester and Winchester respectively; and under their vigorous leadership the south of England was soon covered with Benedictine monasteries.

The saint cared for the people as a father for his children. One practical measure he introduced was to order gold or silver pegs to be fastened to the drinking jugs in taverns. This reminded people not to drink more than their just measure and greatly reduced drunkenness and quarrels.

He could be strict, too, when the occasion demanded it. Once three false coiners were caught and sentenced to have their hands cut off. On that day, which was the Feast of Pentecost, the saint was going to celebrate the Divine Liturgy; but he waited, asking whether the sentence had been carried out. The reply came that the sentence had been deferred to another day out of respect for the feast. "I shall on no account go to the altar today," he said, "until they have suffered the appointed penalty; for I am concerned in this matter." For the criminals were in his power. As he spoke, tears gushed down his cheeks, witnessing to his love for the condemned men. But when they had been punished, he washed his face and went up to the altar, saying: "Now I am confident that the Almighty will accept the Sacrifice from my hands."

Nun's Door, Romsey Abbey

Once the saint was rapt up to heaven in vision,

and saw his mother being married to a great king amidst the joyful chanting of the heavenly hosts. After this had continued for some time, one of the singers, a young man clothed in a shining white garment, came up to Dunstan and said: "Ho is it that you see and hear this multitude glorifying the great king, while you, who ought to be especially joyful at the marriage of your mother remain silent?" Dunstan replied that he did not know the chants that were being sung, nor did he know how he could glorify the king. The young man said: "Do you wish me to instruct you how to chant?" When Dunstan humbly replied that he did, the young man taught him the antiphon: "O King and Lord of all nations, for the sake of the throne of Thy majesty grant unto us the forgiveness of our sins, O Christ our King. Alleluia." This antiphon was repeated several times in the vision until it was firmly established in the saint's memory. And immediately he awoke he ordered a monk to write down what he had so recently learned. Then he commanded all those in obedience to him, both monks and clergy, to learn it. Thus did the saint learn to glorify with chants and spiritual songs the marriage between Christ and his Mother, the Holy Church.

On another occasion, the king asked the saint to postpone the beginning of the Divine Liturgy until he had returned from hunting. The third hour was approaching, and the man of God was standing clad in his hierarchical vestments, immersed in tearful prayer. Suddenly he fell into a light slumber and was rapt up to heaven, where he heard the angels singing: "Kyrie eleison, Christe eleison, Kyrie eleison." Coming to himself, he asked whether the king had arrived. The answer was that he had not. Again he prayed, and again he was rapt up to heaven, where he heard the last words of the Liturgy being pronounced in a high voice. At that moment some clergy ran up to him and told him that the king had arrived. But he replied that he had already been present at the Liturgy, and would not be present at or celebrate it again that day. On being asked why, he revealed to them his vision, after which he forbade the king to hunt again on the Lord's Day. Then he taught the clergy the "Kyrie eleison" which he had heard in the heavens.

Once a nobleman entered into an uncanonical marriage, and when he refused to renounce it, Dunstan excommunicated him. The earl then went to Rome, where he obtained from the Pope a written order to the archbishop compelling him to allow the marriage. But Dunstan, as his name ["firm rock"] implied, was firm as a rock: "I am not to be moved," he said, "even by the threat of death, from the authority of my Lord." In this way the saint demonstrated his truly Orthodox consciousness and freedom from the papist heresy that sought to place the Pope's authority above that of the Universal Church. Nor did the king persuade him to disobey the King of kings and Lord of lords, Jesus Christ. Eventually, the nobleman repented and appeared before Dunstan barefoot and with a candle in his hand; whereupon he was released from his ban.

Now in the capital city of Winchester opposition arose against the monastic reforms which St. Ethelwold, backed by St. Dunstan, was introducing. The secular clergy decided to refer the matter to the king, who in turn referred it to the saint. Dunstan then asked the king to convene a council in Winchester, which met in the refectory of the Old Minster in the presence of the king and queen, the nobles, monks and clergy. The final decision was announced by St. Dunstan: "This Old Minster was founded as a habitation for monks. Let those who benefit from its revenues live henceforth live as true monks." It is said that during the council, when the possibility of restoring the secular clergy to the Old Minster was being discussed, a cross spoke from the wall: "Far be it from you! You have done well: to change again would be wrong."

However, the secular party did not leave it at that. When King Edgar died in 975, and the throne passed to his young son Edward, a great storm arose against the monks in many parts of the country, and the secular clergy who had been expelled from the Old Minster used the council convened at Calne in 977 to renew their complaint. But Dunstan was not to be moved. "Since, in my old age," he said, "you exert yourselves in the stirring up of old quarrels, I confess that I refuse to give in, but commit the cause of His Church to Christ the Judge." His words were confirmed by God's verdict. For as he spoke the house was suddenly shaken; the floor of the upper room in which they were assembled fell under their feet; and the enemies of the Church were thrown to the ground and crushed by the falling timber. Only the beam on which the saint was sitting did not move.

The climax of this time of troubles came with the murder of King Edward in 979. St. Dunstan was greatly saddened by the death of his beloved spiritual son, and, at the coronation of his half-brother, Ethelred, at Kingston, he prophesied great sorrow for the English people in the coming reign. The prophecy was exactly fulfilled after Dunstan's death.

Further sorrows awaited him. In 984, St. Ethelwold and the bishop of Rochester came to visit him at Canterbury. He received them with great joy; but when they were about to return to their sees, he burst into tears, and his weeping was so intense that he could hardly speak. The bishops were terrified by this unusual behaviour, and asked him the reason. After a pause he replied: "I weep because I know that you will soon die." "Don't prophesy such terrible things, most holy father," they said, "for we shall not die, but shall see each other safe and sound another time." But Dunstan confirmed his previous words, saying: "What I have said will come to pass; for you will die to this world but live to God. Nor must you remain any longer in this life, but you will go to God to reign with Him forever." The bishops returned to their sees, sobered by a pious fear of God. Within a few days they both reposed in peace.

As archbishop, Dunstan continued to care for the western monasteries which he had founded or restored. Once he came to the monastery at Bath, where he was charitably received by the brethren. After lunch, he was rapt up in a vision and saw one of the pupils of the nearby Glastonbury school being borne away into the heavens amidst a great host of the heavenly citizens. The next day, a certain Ceolwy came from Glastonbury to ask his blessing and seek his advice on certain problems to do with the monastery and the brethren. When the saint had given him his blessing, he asked him kindly whether everything was well with the brethren. Ceolwy replied that everything was well, completely forgetting about the boy's death. But Dunstan gently said: "I do not suppose that everything could be well for all of you if someone has died." Then Ceolwy replied: "Everything is indeed well, except that one of our boys died yesterday at noon." "That is what I was saying," said the archbishop. "May his spirit rest in peace in accordance with the vision we have been granted."

On another occasion he was staying at Glastonbury and walking with a certain monk named Elfsige near the western gates of the Old Church. Suddenly he heard a voice from heaven, saying: "Come, Elfsige, come." Then, turning to the monk, he said: "Hurry, prepare yourself, brother; for today you have been called by the Lord to leave this world and go to Him." The prophecy was fulfilled a few days later.

The saint was constant in prayer and vigil, and when the first light of any day could be seen, he often applied himself to the correcting of errors in manuscripts. During the day, he would give judgement between man and man, or resolve quarrels, or support widows, orphans and strangers in their necessities. He loved to tell stories from the lives of the saints (the martyrdom of St. Edmund was a particular favourite of his), speaking in both Latin and English. Everyone, including visitors from overseas, was enriched by his holy counsel. And during the Divine Liturgy he would pray with eyes and hands directed to heaven and tears streaming down his cheeks.

But now it came for the man of God to go the way of all flesh.

On the eve of the Feast of the Ascension, 988, a priest of the saint's monastic family at Canterbury, the future bishop of Elmham, Elfgar "the Almsgiver", had the following vision. Dunstan was sitting on his episcopal throne, dictating canon law to a scribe. While he was intent on these things, a great host of heavenly beings was seen entering the church through all the entrances. They surrounded the bishop with their festal array and cried: "Rejoice, our Dunstan! If you are ready, come, join our fellowship as a most honoured member." But he said: "You know, holy spirits, that I must preach to the assembled people in the mother church and communicate them in the Holy Mysteries of the Lord. So I cannot possibly come." To which they replied: "Be ready to come to us on the Sabbath."

On the Feast of the Ascension, two days before

the Sabbath, the saint preached three sermons whose power and glow was wonderful. Then, having said farewell for the last time to his cathedral family, he suddenly felt weak and retired to his bed. And on the morning of the Sabbath, when the Mattins hymns were finished, he told the brethren to come to him. In their presence he commended his spirit to God and received the Holy Mysteries, which had been celebrated on the holy table in his presence. Then, giving thanks to God, he began to chant the words of David: "He made a remembrance of His wondrous deeds; merciful and compassionate is the Lord; He hath given food to them that fear Him." With these words he rested in peace.

St. Dunstan was buried with great honour in Christchurch, Canterbury. Very soon, miracles were being wrought at his tomb. A woman who had been blind for many years was healed after watching and praying at his tomb. A priest was cured of paralysis at his tomb. But a little later, while he was celebrating and giving thanks to God and St. Dunstan, he said: "And if there had been no Dunstan, I should still have been cured." Immediately he was struck with his former paralysis, and died not long after. A boy who had been dumb and lame from his birth was cured at the tomb of the saint. "Glory to God in the highest. Alleluia," were his first words, and he continued to extol the miracle for the rest of his life. A girl who had been blind from her birth was brought to the tomb of the saint by her mother. When her eyes were opened she leapt for joy and said: "Mother, what are these beautiful things which I see?" "Do you see something, my darling?" asked the mother. "A beautiful man commanded me to see these beautiful things," she said. A certain German named Clement had been excommunicated for certain sins, and had been dragged from place to place for seven years, possessed by a demon. Coming to the tomb of the saint, he attended the all-night vigil. At the response, "You see a miracle," he leapt up and vomited the demon out together with some blood.

In the year 1012, a controversy arose between the communities of Canterbury and Glastonbury as to which of them possessed the bones of the saint. The argument was finally settled in 1508, when Archbishop Wareham found the saint's coffin at Canterbury with the inscription: "Here rests St. Dunstan." The holy relics were found wrapped in linen and with a very fragrant odour, as of balsam, which testified to the heavenly glory of which the saint had been counted worthy. [14]

ST. ODA 'THE GOOD' OF CANTERBURY (June 2)

OUR holy father Oda was born in East Anglia, of Danish parents. His father had been a soldier in the Great Army that killed the holy martyr-king Edmund, and was opposed to his son's Christian leanings. So Oda left father and mother and all his possessions to attach himself to a pious man named Ethelhelm, who adopted him as his son and taught him the Christian Faith.

Once Ethelhelm and Oda were on a pilgrimage to Rome. Suddenly the elder had a heart-attack. Oda resorted to prayer, and then gave his teacher a cup of wine over which he had made the sign of the Cross. On drinking the wine, Ethelhelm immediately recovered. News of this miracle reached the ears of the king, as a result of which Oda, who was already a priest, was consecrated to the see of Ramsbury in Wiltshire.

This was in about 925. In 936, Oda was sent by King Athelstan to France to negotiate the restoration of Louis, the son of Emperor Charles the Simple, who was then exiled in England. In 937, Bishop Oda was present at the battle of Brunanburgh, where by his prayers King Athelstan's sword was miraculously repaired, thereby saving his life. [15]

In 942, Oda was appointed archbishop of Canterbury , having become a monk at Fleury-sur-Loire shortly before. As archbishop, Oda showed much courage and wisdom. He encouraged monasticism, issued decrees

Recent uncovering of the original foundations of Canterbury Cathedral. Photo: Bill Cross. *Courtesy of London Daily Mail*

promoting good morals and asserted the independence of the Church from secular authorities.

St. Oda was once celebrating the Divine Liturgy with tears as was his custom, when he saw a drop of blood flowing from the consecrated Gifts. Amazed and struck with fear, he called a priest and showed him the miracle secretly. "You should rejoice, highest father," said the priest, "for today Christ the Son of God has honoured you, that He Who is blessed above all should have counted you worthy to see this with your bodily eyes. And now I beseech the power of the ineffable God to return this His Body to its original form." And when he had prayed, he arose, and found it as before, and partook of it with reverence. After the Liturgy, all the poor, the pilgrims, the orphans and the widows were brought together and given food to the glory of that great miracle. [16]

Oda also greatly embellished his cathedral church at Canterbury. He brought to it the relics of St. Wilfrid from the ruins of Ripon Minster (at the same time commissioning the writing of a new life of the saint), and completely renovated and enlarged the structure erected by St. Augustine. It is said that during the repairs to the cathedral, no rain at all fell on the city.

One of his last acts was to consecrate St. Dunstan to the episcopate. For when King Edwy died, and his brother Edgar ascended the throne of Wessex, he immediately recalled Dunstan from exile. And at a witan (parliament) held at Bradford-on-Avon, "by the choice of all Dunstan was consecrated bishop, especially so that he might constantly be in the royal presence on account of his farseeing and prudent counsels." During the service, however, St. Oda paused at the point where the church to which the new bishop is to be appointed is declared, and, to the astonishment of all, named him bishop of the metropolitan see of Canterbury. Quietly resisting the objections of those around him, he said: "I know, dearly beloved, what God has spoken in me." The holy prelate said this through the Holy Spirit, foreseeing the grace that was to fill Dunstan. For although Dunstan, after his consecration, was sent to the see of Worcester, in two years' time he was archbishop of Canterbury. [17]

St. Oda reposed on June 2, 958, being called "the Good" by St. Dunstan, who never passed his tomb without kneeling. He was succeeded by Elfsin, bishop of Winchester, a man of very different character. One day, Elfsin was standing over Oda's tomb, and addressed him, saying: "Behold, O bishop, here you lie prostrate, and I enjoy the rights of victory. While you were alive I did not obtain them, but now that you are dead, I have taken them." Then he disdainfully struck the tomb with his staff and went away. That same night, the weather was very bad. And St. Oda, clothed in hierarchical vestments, appeared to a certain priest and said to him: "Go to the bishop and diligently ask him why he mocked me yesterday and struck me with his staff." On awaking, however, the priest forgot the words of the saint. Again St. Oda appeared to him and repeated the same words. Again the priest kept silent out of fear. On the third night the saint came to him and reproached him for his slothfulness, adding: "If you wish to preserve the prosperity of this sweet life of yours that you now enjoy, tell your bishop what you have heard." Taking courage from the saint's words, the priest went to the bishop, prostrated himself at his feet, and said: "There came to me, not Gabriel, the Virgin's messenger, but that glorious Oda, your predecessor, who ordered me to say these words to your Eminence with indignation: 'Since you despised me yesterday in word and deed, I tell you that you will cross the sea and climb the mountains, but in no wise will you sit upon the apostolic throne.'" The bishop dismissed this as an idle dream. But the prophecy was fulfilled to the letter: on his way to Rome to receive the pallium, Elfsin caught cold in the Alps and died. [18]

THE UNCOVERING OF THE RELICS OF
ST. SWITHUN
(July 15)

THE holy bishop of Winchester, Swithun, who had been the childhood instructor of King Alfred, reposed on July 2, 862, and was buried just outside the west door of the Old Minster. For over a hundred years, his memory was forgotten, and, as he had wished, people walked over his grave on their way to church without knowing who it was they were stepping on. But the Lord did not wish this light to remain hidden under a bushel; and on July 15, 971 his relics were translated into the cathedral to the accompaniment of a greater outpouring of miracles than had ever been seen in Orthodox England.

About twenty years later, this event was recorded by Abbot Alfric in an account that gives a vivid picture of tenth-century English life:- "For three years before the saint was translated into the church from the stone coffin which now stands inside the new building, he appeared in a vision to a certain faithful blacksmith, wonderfully arrayed, and said: 'Do you know the priest Edsige, who with the other priests was driven out of the old monastery by Bishop Ethelwold for their misconduct?' The smith then answered the venerable Swithun as follows: 'I knew him long ago, sir, but he left this place, and I do not know for certain where he is living now.' Then the holy man said again to the old smith: 'He is now living in Winchcombe. This is the truth. And now I adjure you in the name of Christ: go quickly and give this message, that Swithun the bishop has commanded him to go to Bishop Ethelwold and say that he must himself open my grave and bring my bones inside the church; for he has been counted worthy that in his time I should be made known to men.' Then the smith said to him: 'O sir, Edsige will not believe my words.' Then the bishop said again: 'Let him go to my grave and pull a ring out of the coffin; and if the ring yields at the first tug then he will know for certain that I have sent you to him. If the ring will not come away easily, then he will by no means accept what I say. And after that tell him that he must amend his ways in accordance with the will of the Lord, and hasten singlemindedly to eternal life. And tell everyone that as soon as they open my grave they will find such a valuable hoard that their precious gold will be as nothing by comparison.' Then holy Swithun vanished from the smith's sight.

"However, he did not dare to tell anyone about this vision, fearing to be regarded as an untruthful messenger. So the holy man spoke to him again, and yet a third time, and severely reproved him for not acting in obedience to his commands. Then at last the smith went to his burial-place, and, albeit fearfully, took hold of a ring, crying out to God: 'O Lord God, the Creator of all things, grant me, a sinner, to pull this ring out of the lid, if he who spoke to me three times in a dream is really lying here inside.' Then he pulled the iron out of the stone as easily as if it had stood in sand, and wondered greatly at what had happened. Then he put it back in the hole and pressed it in with his foot. Again it stuck so firmly that no one was able to pull it out. The smith went away awestruck, and in the marketplace he met a serf of Edsige's, to whom he related exactly what Swithun had commanded him, earnestly beseeching him to report it to his master.

"The serf consented, but at first did not dare to tell his master, until he felt that no good would come from concealing the saint's command. Then he told him in order what Swithun had commanded. Now at that time Edsige avoided Bishop Ethelwold and all the monks who were in the minster because of his ejection by them. So he did not obey the saint's command, although the saint was a blood-relative of his. Within two years, however, he retreated to that same monastery, and by the grace of God became a monk, continuing there until he departed this life. Blessed is Almighty God, Who humbles the proud while exalting the humble to high estate, and corrects the sinful while always preserving the good who hope in Him.

"Again, there was certain poor peasant, awfully hunch-backed and bent over in consequence, to whom it was revealed in a dream that he would obtain bodily health and recovery from his crippled state at Swithun's sepulchre. And so he arose joyfully in the morning, crept on two crutches to Winchester and sought the saint as he had been instructed, praying for his health on bended knee. Then he was healed by the holy bishop, so that no trace of the hump which had oppressed him could be seen. At that time the monks did not know about St. Swithun, thinking that some other saint had healed the man. But the peasant said that it was Swithun who had healed him, for he knew best about the matter.

"A certain man was afflicted with a very distressing disease, so that he could hardly open his eyes, or utter a word, but lay in torment thus, despairing of his life. Then all his friends wanted to carry him to the New Minster, to [the relics of] St. Judoc, so that he could recover his health there. But someone told them that it would be better for them to take the sick man to the Old

Minster, to Swithun's grave. This they did, and that night they kept vigil at the grave with him, praying to Almighty God to grant the sick man health through St. Swithun. The sick man also watched until daybreak. Then he fell asleep, and it seemed to all of them as if the tomb was rocking, while to him it seemed as if someone was dragging one of his shoes off his feet. Suddenly he awoke, healed by the holy Swithun. They looked carefully for the shoe, but no one could find it. So they returned home with the man who had been healed.

"Through the power of God eight sick men were miraculously healed at the holy tomb before the body was removed from it.

"After these signs, King Edgar desired the holy man's exhumation, and told the venerable Ethelwold to translate it with great pomp. Then Bishop Ethelwold, accompanied by abbots and monks, took up the saint and bore him into the church of St. Peter. There he remains in honour, working miracles. Then within three days four sick men were healed by the holy man; and there were few days within the next five months in which at least three sick people were not healed — sometimes five or six, or seven or eight, ten or twelve, sixteen or eighteen. Within ten days two hundred men had been healed, and so many within twelve months that no one could count them. The cemetery was filled with cripples, so that people could hardly get into the minster. And within a few days they were all so miraculously healed that one could not find a sick man in the whole of that vast crowd.

"At that time there lived in the Isle of Wight three women, two of whom had been blind for nine years, and the third had never seen the light of the sun. With some difficulty they obtained a dumb guide and came to the saint, and watched there for one night, and were healed, both the blind women and the dumb guide. Then the boy told the sacristan, saying that he had never been able to speak before, and asking for the appointed hymn of praise to be sung.

"At about the same time a certain bondwoman was caught and sentenced to be flogged for some very minor fault. She was put in custody until the morning, when she was to be severely beaten. All night she lay awake, weeping and calling on the holy Swithun to help her, the wretched one, praying that through the power of God he would deliver her from the cruel stripes. When dawn broke, and they began to sing the Praises, the fetters on her feet suddenly fell off, and she ran, with hands still bound, to the church and the blessed saint, in accordance with his will. Then her lord came after her and freed her, loosing her bonds, for the sake of St. Swithun.

"A certain nobleman had lain crippled by paralysis for many years, being unable to move from his bed. Then he said that he wanted to travel to Winchester, if only in his horse-litter, and pray for his healing. While he was saying this to his servants and friends, he was cured. Nevertheless, he made his way to the saint on foot, travelling in front of the company for the whole journey, and earnestly thanked the saint for his recovery." [19]

Twenty-five men suffering from various diseases came to the saint, imploring him to help them. Some were blind, some lame, some deaf and some dumb, and they were all healed in one day through the saint's intercession.

There was a certain very rich nobleman who went suddenly blind. Then he travelled to Rome, wishing to pray to the holy apostles for his cure. For four whole years he stayed in Rome, but was not cured.

Then he heard of St. Swithun, and of the miracles he had wrought since the nobleman had left England. Travelling back in haste, he came to the holy man and was healed there, returning home with perfect sight.

"Another man," continues Abbot Alfric, "had been blind for seven whole years. He had a guide who led him everywhere. One day he went out, but the guide became angry and left him. At a loss how to return home, the blind man cried out to God and St. Swithun in great anguish. He was immediately healed and returned home joyfully without a guide, for which his relatives thanked God fervently.

"Then the venerable and blessed Ethelwold, who was the bishop of Winchester at that time, commanded all the monks who were living in the monastery to go in procession to the church and praise the saint with hymns, and in this way to magnify God because of the great saint every time a sick man was healed. This they did immediately and sang the Te Deum so often — sometimes three, sometimes four times in a night — that they came to hate getting up to do this, as they wanted to go on sleeping. At length they gave up the chanting altogether, for the bishop was busy with the king and had no means of knowing that they were not chanting the Te Deum continually. Then St. Swithun himself came, wonderfully adorned, to a certain good man, and said, 'Go now to the Old Minster and tell the monks that God very much dislikes their murmuring and sloth, for they see God's wonders among them every day but will not praise Christ with chanting as the bishop told the brethren to do. And tell them that if they do not sing the hymn, immediately the miracles will cease. However, if they sing the Te Deum every time a miracle is performed and a sick man healed, then so many miracles will be wrought among them that no one will be able to remember so many miracles having been wrought in his lifetime by anyone.: Then the man awoke from that joyous sleep, lamenting that he could no longer see the bright light which he had seen around Swithun. He arose, however, and went quickly to Bishop Ethelwold, and told him all that had happened. Ethelwold then immediately sent from the king's court to the monks, and told them to sing the Te Deum as he had commanded, with the warning that anyone who neglected this would heavily atone for it by seven days' continuous fasting. From that time they always observed this custom, as we ourselves have very often seen; for we have not infrequently sung this hymn with them.

"A certain man was unjustly accused of stealing, and sentenced to having his eyes put out and his ears cut off. He was immediately seized and the sentence carried out. Then the blood ran down into his head so that he could not hear, and he continued blind and deaf for seven months. Until, that is, he went in faith to St. Swithun, and sought out his relics, and prayed to him that he would at least receive his hearing; for he did not believe that he would ever recover his sight. And he said that he had been unjustly punished in this way. Then through Swithun's intercession a wonder of God was wrought in that man so that he saw clearly with perfect eyes, although they had been thrust out of their sockets and one ball removed entirely, while the other hung down his cheek. He was also granted good hearing — he who had formerly possessed neither eyes nor hearing.

"However, we should understand that we should not pray to God's saints as to God Himself, for He alone is God and above all things; but we should truly pray to the saints to intercede with the omnipotent God, Who is their Lord, that He may come to our aid.

"Once some men were keeping vigil beside a corpse in the customary manner, when a fool, as if in jest, told them with unseemly laughter that he was Swithun. 'You may know that I am in fact Swithun who work these miracles, and it my will that you bring your candles to me and prostrate yourselves, and I shall grant you your desire.' He foolishly blasphemed in this way for a long time until he suddenly fell to the ground, silenced, and as if dead. Immediately they carried him home to his bed, where he lay for a long time, confessing that he had presumptuously spoken foolish words, and asking for forgiveness from the saint. And by the saint's intercession he was healed...

"A certain nobleman's servant had a sudden fall from his horse, so that his arm and left leg were broken. And he was so crushed that he immediately thought that he would die. He had been previously very dear to the lord, and the lord was in great sorrow for his servant, and besought the Almighty from his inmost heart to help the man through the great Swithun. And he also appealed to Swithun, crying out in sorrow: 'O holy Swithun, pray to Jesus that He may grant life to this sick servant. If He does this through you, I shall be more faithful to the living God all the days of my life.' Then the servant arose, made whole through St. Swithun. Then the lord rejoiced, and with faith gave praise to God.

"A certain old nobleman in the Isle of Wight had lain bedridden for some nine years, and could not leave his bed without being carried. Two shining saints appeared to him in a dream and told him to run with them quickly. The sick man said: 'How can I run with you when it is nine years now that I have been unable to rise from this bed alone, without men's help?' Then the saints said: 'If you go with us now, you will come to that place where you will receive healing.' Then he was very glad, and wanted to go with them; and when he found himself unable to travel with them, they flew through the air and carried him until they came to a solitary field with brightly blooming flowers. And standing in the field was a church made of shining gold and precious stones. And St. Swithun stood before the altar, dressed in shining eucharistic vestments, as if about to celebrate the Divine Liturgy. Then Swithun said to the sick man: 'I tell you, brother, from this time forth you must do evil to no man, nor curse any man, nor speak evil of any man, nor be malicious, nor agree with murderers, nor connive at wicked robbers and thieves, nor join in evil deeds, but rather, as best you can, help the needy with your own goods. Then you will be healed by the power of God.' Then the sick man reflected that he did not wish to do evil except to those who had done evil to him, and that he wished to do good to those who had done good to him. But St. Swithun knew the reasoning of his heart, and said to him cheerfully: 'Brother, I tell you, you must not do what you are thinking and harm any man, even if harms you, but imitate your Lord, Who would not curse those who put Him to death, and commanded His followers to pray for their enemies. In the same way Paul the Apostle says to all Christians: "If your enemy hungers, feed him, or if he thirsts, give him to drink."' Then the bedridden man said to the bishop: 'O sir, tell me what kind of man you are, since you are so well able to discern the thoughts of men.' Then St. Swithun said: 'I am he who has just recently come', as if he said: 'I have just recently been made known.' 'What is your name?' asked the man. 'When you come to Winchester, you will know my name,' replied the saint. Then the man was immediately brought back to his bed, and awoke from sleep, and told his wife the whole of the vision he had seen. Then the woman said to him that it was Swithun who had instructed him and whom he had seen looking so glorious in the church. 'It would be very good if some men carried you to church,' she said, 'and if you prayed to the saint to cure you.' Then they immediately carried him from his bed to a church in the Isle of Wight, and he was instantly healed. And he went home whole and on his feet — he who had been carried on a bier to the church. After that he went very quickly to Winchester and told the venerable Bishop Ethelwold how he had been healed through St. Swithun. And Landferth the foreigner wrote it down in Latin...

"A certain Winchester man became angry with his serf because of some carelessness, and put him in fetters. He sat in the hated bonds for a long time until, with the aid of a staff, he hopped out on one foot and with tears prayed to St. Swithun. The bolt immediately shot out of the fetter and the serf arose, freed by the saint.

"We cannot write," concludes Alfric, "nor recount in words, all the miracles the holy Swithun wrought by the power of God in the sight of the people, both on prisoners and on the sick, to manifest to men that they, like Swithun who now shines out through his miracles, may be counted worthy of the Kingdom of heaven by good works. Both wall of the old church were hung, from end to end, with crutches and the stools of cripples who had been healed there. Even so they could not put half of them up..." [20]

ST. EDWARD, THE MARTYR

Icon courtesy of Holy Transfiguraton Monastery

ST. EDWARD THE MARTYR
(March 18)

THE holy Martyr-King Edward was born in about the year 962, the son of King Edgar the Peaceable and his first wife Ethelfleda. On the death of his father, on July 8, 975, he ascended the throne of the English kingdom while still in his teens. There were some who objected to Edward's enthronement, claiming that since neither his father nor his mother were crowned at the time of his birth, it was illegitimate. They wanted to place his half-brother Ethelred, King Edgar's son by his second wife Etheldritha, on the throne in his place. But the controversy was resolved when the archbishop of Canterbury, St. Dunstan, seized the holy Cross that was customarily carried in front of him and, together with other holy bishops, anointed his spiritual son Edward. [21] However, the defeated party of Etheldritha and Ethelred did not give up their opposition to God's chosen one...

Many troubles met the young king on his accession. A great famine was raging, and, beginning in the West and spreading quickly to the East, a violent attack was stirred up against the monasteries by Alderman Elfhere and others, who, according to the Anglo-Saxon Chronicle, "hindered the monastic rule, and destroyed monasteries, dispersed monks, and put to flight God's servants, whom King Edgar had ordered the holy Bishop Ethelwold to establish. Widows were robbed many a time, and many injustices and evil crimes flourished thereafter." [22]

The earliest and most detailed account of the

disturbances was given by the anonymous biographer of St. Oswald, who wrote: "The whole kingdom was thrown into confusion, the bishops were agitated, the noblemen stirred up, the monks shaken with fear, the people terrified. The married clergy were glad, for their time had come. Abbots, with their monks, were expelled, and married clergy, with their wives, introduced; and the last error was worse than the first...And Alderman Elfhere of Mercia, who had acquired great riches, which blind the eyes of many, ejected, on the advice of the people and the outcry of the crowd, not only the sheep, but the shepherds also. Those who used to ride on caparisoned horse, and to join with their fellows in singing the mellifluous chants of King David, you could then see bearing their burden,... or else walking with their companions or friends, without a scrip, without shoes, and thus involuntarily fulfilling the words of the holy Gospel. In those days, if the common crowd spotted a man of our habit, an outcry was raised as if he saw a wolf among the sheep... [However,] it came to pass a few years later that those who had been especially violent against the monks then had neither their own nor others' goods..."[23]

There are hints, in this account, that the monks themselves were not entirely free from blame. "Though some did act rightly, yet many did well," writes the anonymous biographer, who, as a monk of Ramsey, which was in the middle of the troubled area, was in a position to know. Perhaps the "caparisoned horses" annoyed the poor; and it may be that the rich were trying to win back lands which Edgar's monastic benefactions had despoiled them of. [24]

The chief men of the kingdom met to discuss the situation at Kirtlington, Oxfordshire, after Pascha, 977. And here the king and St. Dunstan carried the day, being supported by Alderman Ethelwine of East Anglia, his brother Alfwold, and Alderman Brihtnoth of Essex, the future hero of the battle of Maldon. The tension was such, however, that Bishop Sidemann, the king's tutor, died suddenly during the proceedings. And Alfwold became so furious with one of the men present, who had claimed one of the possessions of Peterborough Abbey as his own, that he had him killed shortly afterwards (he went barefoot to St. Ethelwold in penance for this crime). To cap all this emotion and violence, at another council held in Calne, the floor of the upper storey room in which they were assembled collapsed, and everyone except St. Dunstan (who was sitting on a beam) fell down, many being severely injured.

Peterborough: Remains of the Infirmary

In all this commotion King Edward stood firm in defence of the Church. For this reason certain nobles determined to remove him and replace him by his more amenable younger brother.[25] They seized their opportunity on March 18, 979...

On that day the king was out hunting with dogs and horsemen near Wareham in Dorset. Turning away from this pursuit, he decided to pay a visit to his brother Ethelred, who was being brought up in the house of his mother at Corfe, about three miles from Wareham. He took a small retinue with him, but suddenly, as if playing a joke on him, his retinue broke up and went off in all directions, leaving him to continue on his way alone.

When Etheldritha heard from her servants that the young king was approaching, she hid the evil design in her heart, and went out to meet him in an open and friendly manner, inviting him into her house. But he declined, saying that he only wished to see his brother and talk to him. The queen then suggested that while he was waiting he should have a drink. The king accepted. At that moment one of the queen's party went up to the king and gave him the kiss of peace — a Judas-like gesture, as was soon proved. For as the king was receiving the cup and lifting it to his lips, the man who had kissed him leapt at him from the front and plunged a knife into his body. The king slipped from his saddle and was dragged with one foot in the stirrup until he fell lifeless into a stream at the base of the hill on which Corfe Castle stands.

The queen then ordered the holy body to be seized and thrown into a hut nearby to escape detection. In obedience to her command, her servants took the body by the feet and threw it ignominiously into the hut, concealing it with some mean coverings. Now there lived in that hut a woman blind from birth whom the queen used to support out of charity. While she spent the night there alone with the holy body, suddenly, in the middle of the night, a wonderful light appeared and filled the whole hut. Struck with awe, the poor woman cried out: "Lord, have mercy!" At this, she suddenly received her sight, which she had so long desired. And then, removing the covering which covered the dead king, she discovered his body. The present church of St. Edward at Corfe stands on the site of this miracle.

The stream into which the holy king's body first fell was found to have healing properties, and many pilgrims who washed their eyes in its water recovered or improved their sight, including two reported cases in modern times.

At dawn the next day, when the queen learned of the miracle, she was troubled and decided to conceal the body in a different way. So she ordered her followers to take it up and bury it in a remote marshy place. At the same time she commanded that no one should grieve over the king's death, or even speak about it. Then she retired to a manor in her possession called Bere, ten miles from Corfe.

Meanwhile, such grief took hold of Ethelred over his brother's death that he could not stop weeping. This roused his mother to such fury that she took some candles and beat him with them viciously, hoping thereby to stem the flow of his tears. It is said that thereafter Ethelred so hated candles that he would never allow them to be lighted in his presence.

Almost a year passed, and it pleased Almighty God to make known the heavenly glory of the martyr-king. For a pillar of fire was seen over the place where his body was hidden, lighting up the whole area. This was seen by some devout inhabitants of Wareham, who met together and raised the body from the place where it lay; whence a sweet, clear spring of healing water sprang up. Then, accompanied by a huge crowd of mourners, the body was taken to the church of the Most Holy Mother of God in Wareham and buried at the east end. This first translation of the holy relics took place on February 13, 980.

Meanwhile, the queen's deceit and wickedness were made known throughout the country, the fame of the innocent martyr-king increased, and many signs and miracles testified to his holiness. Alderman Elfhere was overjoyed, and, wishing to make amends for his former evil deeds, — for, in William of Malmesbury's words, "he repented of his rashness, and was deeply distressed in mind"[26] — he decided to have the body translated to a worthier resting-place. Bishops and abbots were invited, together with Abbess Wulfrida and the nuns of Wilton, who included St. Edith, the martyr's half-sister. A great number of laymen and women of Dorset also converged on Wareham.

Then the holy body was disinterred in the presence of the whole people and was found to be completely untouched by corruption. Seeing this, St. Dunstan and the other bishops led the people in hymns of praise to God, while St. Edith ran up to her brother's body and embraced it with tears of joy and sorrow combined. Then the body was lifted onto a bier and with a great procession of clergy and laity was taken to Shaftesbury, to the convent founded by King Alfred the Great in honour of the Most Holy Mother of God. The procession began on February 13, 981, and arrived at Shaftesbury seven days later, on February 20. There the holy body was received by the nuns, and it was buried with great ceremony on the north side of the altar.

On the way, two poor men who were so bent over and paralysed that they could hardly crawl on their hands and knees were brought close to the bier. Those carrying it then lowered the sacred body down to their level, and immediately in the sight of all they were restored to health. A great shout rose to the heavens and all in common gave praise to the holy martyr.

On hearing of the miracles wrought through the saint, the queen was overcome by remorse and decided to go to him to ask for his forgiveness. But as she rode with her followers her horse suddenly refused to go further. Neither by the whip nor by threats could she gain ground, and she realized that she was held back by the force of her sins. She then jumped from the horse and prepared to go on foot; but again she was hurled back and could make no headway. Later, weeping bitterly for her sins, the queen retired to a convent at Wherwell, where "for many years she clothed her pampered body in hair-cloth, sleeping at night upon the ground without a pillow, and mortifying her flesh with every kind of penance". [27]

During the twenty years after the translation of the relics of St. Edward to Shaftesbury, many miracles were wrought at the tomb of the holy king. Thus there was a woman living in a remote part of England, who, weighed down by a great infirmity, daily poured forth prayers for her health. One night St. Edward appeared to her in a dream and said: "When you rise at dawn, go without delay to the place where I am entombed, for there you will receive new shoes necessary for your infirmity." For she had an injury to her feet, and the healing of her feet was signified by "shoes". Waking early, the woman reported the dream she had had to her neighbour; but she, disbelieving the vision, declared that it was imagination. And so the woman disobeyed the command of the saint. But he, appearing to her a second time, said: "Why do you spurn my command and so greatly neglect your health? Go then to my tomb and there you will be delivered." She recovered her strength and said: "Who are you, lord? Where shall I find your tomb?" He replied: "I am King Edward, recently killed by an unjust death and buried at Shaftesbury, in the church of Mary, the blessed Mother of God." The woman woke early, and, thinking over what she had seen, took what was needed for her journey and made her way to the monastery. Arriving there, she prayed for some time with humble heart to God and St. Edward, and was restored to health.

Great miracles continued to be wrought at the tomb of the royal martyr, and in 1001 his brother Ethelred, who had succeeded him on the throne, granted Bradford-on-Avon "to Christ and His saint, my brother Edward, whom, covered in his own blood, the Lord Himself has deigned to magnify by many signs of power." [28]

Bradford-on-Avon: Church of St. Laurence, c. 700

At about the same time the tomb in which the saint lay began to rise from the ground, indicating that he wished his remains to be raised from the earth. In confirmation of this he appeared in a vision to a monk and said: "Go to the convent called by the famous name of Shaftesbury, and take commands to the nun Ethelfreda who is in charge of the other servants of God there. You will say to her that I do not wish to remain any longer in the place where I now lie, and command her on my behalf to report this to my brother without delay." Rising early, and perceiving that the vision he had seen was from God, the monk quickly made his way to the abbess as he had been commanded and told her in order all that had been revealed to him. Then the abbess, giving thanks to God, immediately told the whole story to King Ethelred, at the same time making known to him the elevation of the tomb. The king was filled with joy and would have been present at the elevation if he had been able. But, being prevented by serious incursions of the Danes, he sent messengers to the holy bishops Wulsin of Sherborne and Elfsin of Dorchester-on-Thames, as well as to other men of respected life, instructing them to raise his brother's tomb from the ground and replace it in a fitting place. Following the king's command, those men joyfully assembled at the monastery with a vast crowd of laymen and women. The tomb was opened with the utmost reverence; and such a fragrant smell issued from it that all present thought that they stood among the delights of Paradise. Then the holy prelates came near, bore away the sacred relics from the tomb, and, placing them in a casket carefully prepared for this, carried it in procession to the holy place of the Saints together with other relics. This elevation of the relics of St. Edward took place on June 20, 1001.

Dorchester Abbey: Jesse Window

St. Edward was officially glorified by an act of the All-English Council of 1008, presided over by the hieromartyr archbishop of Canterbury, St. Alphege; and

King Ethelred ordered that three of his feastdays (March 18, February 13 and June 20) should be celebrated throughout England. A part of the relics were later removed to Leominster and Abingdon. The convent church was rededicated to the Mother of God and St. Edward, and that part of the town was called Edward-stowe.

Many miracles continued to be wrought at the tomb of St. Edward. Thus during the reign of King Edward the Confessor a man named John living in northwest France, whose whole body had been so bent by severe pain that his heels were touching his loins and he was unable to stand upright, was told in a vision at night to journey to England to the monastery at Shaftesbury where St. Edward lay, as there he would recover his health. He recounted this to his neighbours and relatives, and relying on their help and advice he crossed the Channel and after many detours at last reached the convent. Having prayed there for some time to God and St. Edward, he recovered his health, and remained as a servant at the monastery for the rest of his life.

Not long after, a leper came to the tomb of the saint, and after invoking God's help by prayers and vigils, he received complete cleansing from his infirmity. Another man who had been bound in heavy chains for his sins was suddenly freed from them as he was praying earnestly at the tomb. Again, Bishop Herman of Salisbury was staying at the monastery, and a poor blind man whom he supported was with him. While the bishop was tarrying, the blind man decided to go and pray at the tomb, led by a boy who guided his steps. He continued praying until evening, when the wardens who were looking after the church asked him to leave. He refused, and said that he would wait on the mercy of God and St. Edward. Impressed by his faith, they let him stay, while making the boy return to his lodging. After staying quietly at his place for some time, the blind man was overwhelmed first by extreme cold, then by extreme heat. And then he recovered his sight. The next morning, some would not believe the miracle; but when witnesses came forward who affirmed that he had been blind for a long time, praise was given to Christ Who works great wonders through His saints.

In the twelfth century, it was reported that King Edward's lung still quivered. And in 1904 an eleventh-century glass vessel containing a "shrunken nut-like object" was found beneath a small marble slab in the centre of the foot-pace, in front of the High Altar. The vase may still be seen in Winchester Cathedral, but the relic, which may well have been St. Edward's lung, was thrown away.

Miracles continued to be reported at the abbey site even in modern times. And in the early 1930s the relics of the saint were discovered in the North Transept of the abbey. On September 3, 1984 (Orthodox calendar; September 16 according to the new calendar), the relics were translated to the Orthodox Church of St. Edward at Brookwood, near Guildford. [29]

ST. ETHELWOLD OF WINCHESTER (August 1)

OUR holy Father Ethelwold was born in Winchester in about the year 912. When he was still in his mother's womb, as Abbot Alfric relates, "it seemed to her that she was sitting in front of the door of her house and that she saw a lofty banner whose top seemed to touch the sky. Bowing reverently, it surrounded the pregnant woman with its fringes. Similarly, while she was sleeping that same night, she saw as it were a golden eagle come out of her mouth and fly away. It was so big that the whole city seemed to be shadowed by its gilded wings."[30]

The child was baptized and called Ethelwold. Once, on a certain feast day, his mother was at home holding the child in her lap. She wanted to go to church, but a wind arose that was so strong that she was unable to fulfill her intention. Then she set about praying earnestly. And suddenly she found herself sitting with the child in church during the Divine Liturgy.

As a boy, he was introduced into the court of King Athelstan, where he learned many useful things. But his mind was set on heavenly things. And so he was at length ordained a priest together with St. Dunstan by the bishop of Winchester, St. Alphege.

After a period of instruction under St. Alphege, Ethelwold submitted himself in obedience to St. Dunstan at Glastonbury. There he worked as a cook, learned grammar and studied the Fathers; fasted, prayed and kept vigil with zeal; and, after being raised to the position of prior, continually exhorted the brethren to higher things. He remained in obedience to St. Dunstan until his death.

It was while Ethelwold was prior of the monastery at Glastonbury that St. Dunstan had a prophetic dream about him. Wulfstan, a pupil of Ethelwold's at Winchester, relates that Dunstan was sitting outside the monastery dormitory when he saw "a certain tree as it were of wondrous height. It seemed to spread its branches east, west, north, and south, over the entire region of Britain, astonishingly extensive in its length and breadth. The branches of this tree were laden with countless cones, large and small, while the tree itself bore at the very top a huge cone which, rising above, protected the others with the covering of its scales, and surpassing them all together with its great height, touched the very sky. But the man of the Lord, Dunstan, very astonished by such a vision from above, questioned the elder adorned with white angelic hair, who was pointing this tree out to him, and said: 'I beseech you, venerable elder, what is this strong and lofty tree whose branches spreading out far and wide seem to support so many countless cones?' The elder answered him: 'This tree which you see, Abbot Dunstan, represents the site of this island; moreover, the great cone which rises on the pinnacle of this tree represents your monk Ethelwold who serves Christ devoutly in this monastery. Now the other cones with which these branches appear laden represent the multitude of monks who are to be instructed by his learning and who are to be gathered together in this area from all regions for the service of Almighty God. Under his leadership they will reach the glory of the Kingdom of heaven and the fellowship of the blessed spirits who reign with Christ.' Having received this reply, the holy man awoke and reflected silently upon the vision, and afterwards made it known to the faithful by a true account. The report of the vision, spreading with the passage of time, became known to many and at length came also to my humble notice.

"And it was also no less fitting," continues Wulfstan, "that another dream be fulfilled which Ethelwold, the holy man of God, once related to me concerning himself, saying: 'I thought that I was standing by the sea shore where it seemed to me that there appeared a certain great ship, in which there was contained a plentiful number of fish, especially eels, heaped up from the bottom to the top. And when I silently considered the meaning of this vision which I saw, I suddenly heard a voice calling me by my own name, and saying to me: "Ethelwold, Ethelwold, this command has been sent to you by God from heaven: Call forth those fish, with which the ship that you perceive is filled, and bring it about by your prayers that they may be men, just as they were before." Thereupon, complying with this command I stood before them to pray and overcome with a shower of tears, I said sighing: "Lord Jesus, for Whom nothing is impossible, look favourably upon these souls deceived by diabolical trickery, who have been alienated from the slimy mud of this world. I beseech Thee, Good Jesus, do not allow the enemy of the human race to glory in his triumph over them, but grant that, through the almighty power of Thy Name, they may be restored to life, so that, escaping the sleep of eternal death, they may acknowledge Thee as the true and only Saviour of the world, and thereafter, always fleeing towards the peaceful gate of Thy salvation, may be rescued from all dangers of the world and remain secure under Thy governance. For it is Thine, O Christ, to make the dead live, and to restore to its former glory

Thine own image which Thou hast created. Thou camest into this world to save sinners and having suffered the dreadful punishment of death on the cross, thou didst deign to pour forth Thy precious blood for the salvation of us all." When I uttered these and similar words of prayer with a remorseful heart and spirit of humility, behold the fish which I had seen before covered in the filthy mud and in the waters of misery, I suddenly saw made into men and revived from death. There arose from the ship and proceeded hastily to land a great multitude of men, many of whom I had known personally. One man among them who fell behind was transformed again into an eel. Without doubt he was that Athelstan, who had long ago been ordained priest with me, and whom thereafter I had been unable to rouse by any means or to bring it about that he might become a man.[31] Indeed all the others with one accord raised their voices to heaven, clapping their hands and offering thanks to Almighty God because through His ineffable mercy and my insignificant coming, they were worthy to be recalled from death to life and to be restored to human reasoning which they had lost. But I, rejoicing in God and wishing them joy, awoke, and thus I recall this vision for you, my children, so that with the labour of good works you may persevere in the holy purpose; whereby, through the grace of God, you are able to be counted in the number of those who have been entrusted to me, although I am unworthy, so that they may be freed from the unclean abyss of this world and be saved in eternal blessedness without end.'" [32]

After some time, the saint wished to go overseas to learn more about the monastic life. However, the Dowager-Queen Edith, King Edred's mother, was against this (Ethelwold later sent the monk Osgar to Fleury instead of himself); and she persuaded her son to give Ethelwold the derelict monastery at Abingdon, together with a large area of land to support it. And so, with St. Dunstan's blessing, the saint went to Abingdon, and set about reconstructing the monastery. Soon monks came to him from all around, from Glastonbury, Winchester and London. Then he was ordained as abbot over them at the king's request.

Once, as Abbot Alfric relates, "the king came to the monastery to plan himself the structure of the buildings, and he measured out all the foundations of the monastery with his own hand, exactly as he had determined to erect the walls. Then the abbot invited him to dine in the refectory with his men. The king agreed immediately; and since there were several Northumbrians with him at the time, they all came with the king to the feast. The king was merry, and ordered mead to be supplied in abundance to the guests, having closed the doors so that no one could hurry away and leave the drinking at the royal banquet. The whole day the servers drew drink for the revellers in full measure, and yet a span's depth remained until the Northumbrians were swinishly drunk and withdrew in the evening." [33]

Once a brother named Elfstan (the future Bishop Elfstan I of Ramsbury) was ordered by the saint to provide food for the builders of the monastery. He very zealously prepared meat every day for the workmen, and personally served them, kindling the hearth, fetching water and cleaning the vessels, while the abbot thought he did all this with the help of a servant. One day, while the abbot was wandering around the monastery as was his custom, he saw Elfstan standing by a boiling cauldron, preparing food for the workmen. And, entering the kitchen, he saw all the vessels spotless and the floor swept. Then he went up to Elfstan, and said joyfully: "My brother, you have robbed me of this obedience which you practise without my knowledge. But if you are as much a soldier of Christ as you seem, put your hand in the boiling water and draw out from the bottom for me a bit of food." Without hesitating, Elfstan put his hand to the bottom of the cauldron and drew out a hot morsel, feeling no heat from the boiling water. When the saint saw this, he ordered Elfstan to put down the food and reveal the miracle to no one.

Another time, the saint was working on the building when a huge post fell on him and threw him into a pit, breaking nearly all his ribs on one side. And if the pit had not received him, he would have been completely crushed. However, he recovered with the help of God; and on November 29, 963, before the building was completed, he was consecrated bishop of Winchester by St. Dunstan at the king's request.

Coming to his see, St. Ethelwold found the Old Minster occupied by evil-living clergy, who often neglected the celebration of the Liturgy, kept concubines, and were given over to gluttony and drunkenness. With King Edgar's permission, he expelled these clerics, and replaced them with monks from Abingdon. "Now it happened," writes Abbot Alfric, "that while the monks who had come from Abingdon were standing at the entrance of the church, the clerics inside were finishing the Divine Liturgy and singing the communion hymn: 'Serve ye the lord with fear, and rejoice in Him with trembling; embrace discipline, lest at any time you perish from the righteous way.' As if they were saying: 'We would not serve God, nor observe His discipline; you at least act so that you do not perish like us.' And the monks, hearing their singing, said one to another: 'Why are we waiting outside? Look, we are exhorted to enter.'" [34]

Abingdon Abbey

St. Ethelwold also came, together with a thegn of King Edgar's named Wulfstan. They gave the clerics the royal ultimatum: either give place to the monks or become monks yourselves. The clerics, no lovers of the monastic life, decided to leave, although three of them, named Edsige, Wulfsige and Wilstan, later accepted the monastic tonsure. [35]

However, the clerics did not give up without a fight. They appealed to the king, who in turn referred the matter to St. Dunstan. Dunstan then asked the king to convene a council at Winchester. This took place in the refectory of the Old Minster in the presence of the king and queen, nobles and clergy. The final decision was announced by St. Dunstan: "This Old Minster was founded as a habitation for monks. Let those who benefit from its revenues live henceforth as true monks." It is said that during the council, when the possibility of restoring the secular clergy to the Old minster was being discussed, a cross spoke from the wall: "Far be it from you! You have done well; to change again would be wrong." [36] Besides this, the Council decided on the establishment of a slightly modified form of the Rule of St. Benedict, the Regularis Concordia, for all the monastics of England. And the monks were to be under the patronage of the king, and the nuns — of the queen.

King Edgar supported Ethelwold's reforms, not only in the Old, but also in the New Minster, as well as in the women's Nunnaminster. "The three abbeys," writes Duckett, "stood on adjoining lands, the New Minster a little to the north of the Old, and the Nuns' Minster on the east. Trouble was constant among them. Terms strictly 30 days. They were jealous of possessions; they disputed thed lines of their boundaries; they declared respectively that they could not sing their office in the proper manner because of the noise of chanting from their monastic neighbours. King Edgar at Aethelwold's petition issued order for exact division among them and even tore down the houses of private citizens near by in order that space might be given to the monks of Winchester 'for living more peacefully in God's service, removed from the clamour of townspeople.' Such action was hard for the townspeople, yet Aethelwold in the end also did them untold good. With extraordinary imagination and practical skill he made his engineers and their workmen conduct a sorely needed supply of water by channels through the streets of Winchester to cloisters and to private homes alike." [37]

Moreover, during a famine, he ordered the treasures of the Church, its silver vessels and fine ornaments, to be broken down to make money for the poor, saying: "What is lifeless metal compared with bodies and souls created and redeemed by God?"

The saint was a great patron of the ecclesiastical arts. He built, according to David Hugh Farmer, "the most powerful organ of its time in England. It was played by two monks and had 400 pipes and 36 bellows. Bells and a crown of metal for candles in the sanctuary at Abingdon were also attributed to him. Even more important was the appearance in Ethelwold's monasteries of the new influential Winchester style of illumination, which soon surpassed in excellence the products of many scriptoria of continental monasteries. His school of vernacular writing at Winchester, of which Aelfric is the most famous example, was the most important of its time; its accurate translations, linguistically significant, were designed to meet the needs of bishops and clergy who were not themselves monks. In music Ethelwold's Winchester had the distinction of producing the first English polyphony in the Winchester Troper." [38]

And if, in musical terms, the saint was something of an innovator, he resisted innovation in other areas — for example, the uncanonical practice, then taking root in the West, of celebrating the Divine Liturgy more than once a day. Thus he once celebrated a Funeral Liturgy, and an hour later one of his monks asked him if he were going to celebrate the normal daily Liturgy. "Have I not offered the Eucharist today?" said the bishop. "Yes, but that was a funeral," replied the monk. "Enough for me," said the bishop. [39]

An inscription in his Benedictional calls him Boanerges, "son of thunder", and he could be very strict to the disobedient. But to the gentle and humble, says Alfric, he was "gentler than a dove... He was a father of the monks and nuns, a comforter of widows and a restorer of the poor, a defender of churches, a corrector of those going astray, for he performed more by his work than we can relate in words." [40]

"He was often," continues Alfric, "afflicted with illness in his bowels and legs, spending sleepless nights from pain, and nevertheless going about by day as if well, though pale. Yet he did not indulge in the flesh of animals and birds except once for three months, when forced by great infirmity — and this, moreover, he did at the command of Archbishop Dunstan — and again during the sickness from which he died. It was always a pleasure to him to teach young men and boys, and to explain books to them in English, and with kindly exhortations to encourage them to better things. From this it came about that several of his pupils were made abbots and bishops in the English people.

"It happened once that his clerk, who had been appointed to carry his ampulla took less oil than was required, and even this he lost on the way. When the bishop came to their destination, and wished to have the chrism, he had none. Very troubled, the clerk then retraced the road he had come, and discovered the ampulla, which before had not been half full, lying full of oil.

"A monk serving him, Edwin by name, stole the purse of a guest, by the instigation of the devil. The bishop spoke to the whole congregation in chapter about this matter, saying that if anyone had taken it he should return it with his blessing, or throw it down in a place where it might be pondering what he ought to do. Yet he had power to move all his limbs except his arms, which the bishop had rendered useless by the power conferred on him by God. However, the wretched man arose thus bound, and going after the bishop, was constrained to confess that he had the thing secretly, saying nothing about his binding. Then the bishop said to him gently, as was his habit: 'At least you have done well in confessing your crime now, although late; have then our blessing.' And immediately his arms were loosed without the bishop knowing. But he went away gladdened by this and told everything about his binding and his release to a certain brother, Wulfgar by name, who advised that this should rather be kept hidden in silence.

"When the bishop wished to restore the old church with great effort, and ordered the brethren frequently to work alongside the workmen, it happened one day that while the monks were standing with the masons on the top of the roof of the church a monk named Goda fell from the top to the bottom. And immediately he touched the ground he got up without having suffered any injury from such a fall, and mounted to the work where he had stood before and seizing a trowel completed what he had begun. To whom therefore ought this miracle to be ascribed unless to him by whose order he went out to this work.

"Also a certain monk, Theodric by name, went to the bishop in the nocturnal interval wishing to inform him by signs about a certain necessary matter, and discovered him reading with a candle, and sharpening his aged eyes by unremittingly blinking his eyelids; and he stood a long time marvelling at how diligently he kept his eyes fixed to the page. Then the bishop rose from his reading and that brother took the candle and began to read, trying if he could sharpen his sound eyes to the reading as diligently as the bishop had done his failing eyes. But that temerity did not go unpunished, for the following night, when he had given himself to sleep, there appeared to him someone of unknown countenance, saying to him with terrible threatening: 'How dared you reproach the bishop in his reading last night?' And, saying this, he struck him a blow in the eyes with his finger, and there immediately followed a violent pain in the eyes which afflicted him greatly for many days, until he obliterated by amends the fault which he had needlessly committed against the holy man.

"Again, it happened that when the bishop was reading he fell asleep from too many vigils, and the burning candle fell on the page and continued to burn on the leaf until a brother arrived and took the flaming candle from the book, and saw the glowing pieces of the candle lying on many lines inside, and when he blew them out he found the page undamaged." [41]

The dedication, in 980, of the reconstructed Old Minster was the occasion for a reconciliation between Saints Dunstan and Ethelwold and the other monastic reformers, on the one side, and the leaders of the anti-monastic reaction in the previous reign, on the other. Thus Wulfstan writes that "it was dedicated solemnly and with great glory by nine bishops, of whom the first and most important, Dunstan the Archbishop, and Ethelwold himself, the holy bishop, took precedence. From the 20th day of October in the presence of King Ethelred and in the assembly of almost all the earls, abbots, aldermen and foremost nobles of the entire English nation, they celebrated for two days that same dedication with universal joy. Thereafter, his heavenly piety brought so much esteem to the holy bishop that those men, distinguished with secular power, princes, dukes, mighty lords, and judges, and all who until now were opposed to him and seemed to stand in the way of God, were suddenly changed as if from wolves into sheep and venerated him with wonderful affection. Bending their necks to their knees and kissing his right hand, they commended themselves in all things to the prayers of the man of God." [42]

Now the time came for St. Ethelwold to depart from this earthly life. Having arrived in a village called Beddington, some sixty miles from Winchester, he fell severely ill, and received the sacraments of Holy Unction and the Body and Blood of the Lord. Then, having said farewell to his spiritual children and blessed them, he reposed on August 1, 984. And "those who were present there," writes Wulfstan, "have testified to me that the dead body of the holy man was altered by a sudden change; it was covered with a milky-white radiance and was made beautiful with a rose-coloured glow. Thus, in a certain way the countenance of a boy seven years old seemed to manifest itself, and then on this countenance a kind of glory of the resurrection appeared through the manifestation of his changed body." [43]

An enormous multitude from all classes of society came from the neighbouring villages and towns to say farewell to their beloved pastor. And when, on the following day, the funeral bier, surrounded by Gospels, crosses and lighted candles, and accompanied by the chanting of psalms and hymns, entered Winchester, the whole city came out to meet the procession. The body of the saint was brought to his own episcopal chair in the cathedral church of SS. Peter and Paul, where a vigil service and Divine Liturgy were celebrated; after which, writes Wulfstan, "he was buried in the crypt on the south side of the holy altar, where long ago it was shown to him from on high that he must rest, as he himself told me." [44]

"Twelve years after the saint's repose," continues Wulfstan, "it pleased God that Ethelwold should be revealed by heavenly signs and his bones taken up from the enclosure of the tomb so that the light, which lay hidden under a bushel might be placed on a lampstand to shine for all those who are in the house of God. For there is a certain small city bustling with commerce that is usually called Wallingford, in which there lived a certain energetic man whose name was Elfhelm. Having lost his sight by accident, he patiently endured blindness for many years. The holy Bishop Ethelwold appeared to this man in his sleep at early dawn and urged him to go quickly to Winchester and to approach his tomb in order to receive the grace of sight, saying: 'Therefore I visit you, lying in your bed, and I foretell the things that will happen to you so that by the sign of your cure it will be clear that I should be raised up from the tomb in which I lie.' When he had heard this and had recognized the voice of the one who was speaking to him, he thanked the holy father because he deigned to visit him. And because Elfhelm was completely ignorant of where Ethelwold was buried, he diligently inquired how he would be able to recognize his tomb and approach it. The man of God immediately revealed to him the name of his former pupil and monk whom the blind man until now did not know, and said to him: "When you arrive in haste at Winchester and enter the church of the old monastery, summon a certain monk, Wulfstan, surnamed the Precentor. When he hears from your mouth the words of my message, he will then without hesitation lead you to my tomb and there you will receive your sight." What more is there to tell? Believing the words and promises of the holy bishop, that man went quickly to Winchester, entered the church, and summoned the aforesaid brother and asked him to grant the request of the holy father and tell him and all present the details of the vision. For it was the evening on which the birth of the most holy Mother of God and ever-virgin Mary is celebrated solemnly and most fittingly throughout the world. In truth, that brother was astonished and, wavering between hope and fear, he humbly submitted to the commands of the holy bishop with obedient steps and led the blind man to the chamber of the tomb. The blind man stayed there through the night in prayer, and when morning came, no longer needing a guide, he returned homewards with joy, having his sight and blessing the Lord with heart and soul.

"This revelation, which had been confirmed by so clear a miracle, was made known far and wide. Thereafter, the servant of Christ appeared clearly to the same brother Wulfstan and to many others in visions by night. Through these and other signs, he revealed himself to them because it was in accordance with the Divine will that he be transferred from his tomb and worthily placed in the church. Therefore, the venerable Bishop Alphege [the future hieromartyr archbishop of Canterbury], Ethelwold's successor, privately studying these matters with keen understanding, rendered humble thanks with a fervent heart to Christ the Almighty because in his own time, he deigned to glorify His saint through His heavenly signs. Without delay, he honourably transferred the remains of the holy Bishop Ethelwold on September 11th and placed them in the choir of the church. There they have been held in great veneration until the present day and there heavenly miracles have been performed even while we behold them. From these I have briefly related two as an indication of his power.

"At that time, there was in the city of Winchester a certain little girl, the daughter of one Ethelworth, who was exceedingly ill and who was tormented almost to death. Led by her mother to the tomb of the man of God, the child went to sleep for a little while and immediately on awakening she rose sound in body, and returned home rejoicing with her mother.

"And likewise a certain little boy, son of one Elfsinus, a quiet and modest man, had been deprived of his sight in his infancy and was brought in his mother's arms to the tomb of the venerable father Ethelwold. It is wonderful to say that the affliction of his blindness thereupon disappeared, and the brightness of light coming forth opened the boy's eyes. All the people rejoiced and in complete devotion gave thanks to Christ.

"Nor must it be passed over in silence that the aforementioned successor of the saint, Bishop Alphege, had ordered a certain thief to be flogged with whips on account of his many offences and to be sent to the stocks to suffer severe punishment. And when the condemned one had for some time lain thus in torment, on a certain night the holy bishop of God, Ethelwold, came to him in a vision and said to him: 'Wretched one, why do you lie thus stretched out in the stocks for so long a time?' But he recognized the holy man whom he had often seen in his mortal life, and replied: 'My lord, I endure a fitting punishment and am tormented thus by the just sentence of the bishop, because often I have been caught stealing and have not ceased from this, but again and again I have repeated the crimes which I committed.' Then the saint said: 'Stop even now, wretched one, stop thieving and be released from the bonds of these fetters.' The wretched man, liberated, immediately arose and departing he went away and fell down before the feet of Bishop Alphege. He told him in order what had happened to him, and for the sake of the honour of so great a father, the bishop allowed him to leave unharmed. Therefore it is certain that this saint, joined to eternal life, is able, by virtue of his merits, to free us from the bonds of our sins and to lead us to the Kingdom of heaven. For while he was still in the body, the power of binding and setting free had been granted to him from heaven by the gift of our Lord Jesus Christ." [45]

ST. EDITH OF WILTON (September 16)

THE holy virgin Edith was born in Kemsing, Kent, of an illicit union between King Edgar and the daughter of an earl of royal blood, Wulfrida.

Edgar wished to make Wulfrida his queen, but she fled to the convent of Wilton, where she received the monastic tonsure from St. Ethelwold. Soon Wulfrida came to excel in virtue, and she was chosen to be spiritual mother of the community. Edith was brought up in the convent under her mother's supervision, and at length she, too, was tonsured with her father's consent. In the convent she learned writing, drawing, sewing and embroidery, and was taught by the two foreign chaplains, Radbod of Rheims and Benno of Treves. She was also influenced by the holy example of her namesake and paternal aunt, Edith of Polesworth, and by her grandmother, St. Elgiva.

St. Edith was distinguished by her abstinence, even on feastdays, and by her love for the poor, the lepers, the blind and the maimed. She dressed in beautiful clothes, but wore a hairshirt next to her skin. Not realizing this secret asceticism, St. Ethelwold once said to her: "My daughter, it is not with such vestments that one goes to the bridal chamber of Christ. Nor does the Heavenly Bridegroom delight in the external beautifying of the body." She replied: "Believe me, father, with God's help the mind is no worse under this covering than under a goatskin. I have my Lord Who looks not so

R. DUCKWORTH

ST. EDITH

much at my clothes as at my mind." The man of God sensed the grace in her words, and did not further reproach her.

Now a serving-woman once left a half-extinguished candle in a chest full of the virgin's clothes. Having bolted the chest, she went away. Soon the smouldering candle generated a dangerous fire in the bedroom, and the wall caught fire. It was night and everyone was asleep; but the unsleeping Providence of God roused the sisters, who came running and tired to break open the chest. They pulled out the burning clothes and extinguished the flames. But when, with the aid of covered lights, they examined the clothes carefully, they were astonished to see that they were all completely untouched. All this time Edith had been quite tranquil and undisturbed, her mind fixed on Christ. The scorched chest was kept in the monastery as a witness to the miracle.

Wherever Edith went, the Cross of Christ was her companion. She made the sign of the Cross on her forehead and chest before every work and while travelling. Once, as she was giving food to the poor, as was her custom, a boy ran up from the side and asked for alms. She gave them to him, making the sign of the Cross at the same time. Immediately the boy disappeared, vanished into thin air — a demonic phantom destroyed by the power of the Cross.

When King Edgar died and her half-brother Edward ascended the throne, Edith had a vision in which she saw the young king's right eye fall out. Relating this to the sisters, she said: "It seems to me that this portends the death of my brother." And so it turned out. After her brother's death, some nobles wanted to make her queen. But she refused.

Edith had a great devotion to St. Dionysius the Areopagite, and she had a wooden church built in his name adjoining the main church of the monastery. It had three entrances with the Cross inscribed over each. The interior was covered by multi-covered frescoes painted by the chaplain Benno. When the church was completed, Edith invited St. Dunstan to consecrate it. During his visit, he saw the holy virgin extend the thumb and first three fingers of her right hand to make the sign of the Cross. [46] Delighted by this, he took her right hand and said: "May this thumb never perish!" A little later, during the celebration of the Divine Liturgy, the holy man broke into tears. And when the deacon asked him why he was weeping, he said: "This soul beloved of God, this heavenly jewel, will be taken from this miserable life and earthly filth to the land of the saints. Nor is this shameful world worthy of such a great light. Forty three days from now this brilliant star will depart from us. Behold how the lights of the saints are taken from this our prison while we sit in the darkness and shadow of death. Her immature age condemns our slothful senility, and while we sleep, she enters into the marriage with her lamp full of oil, and takes before us the beauty of the crown. Now thou goest to a better age, O blessed citizen of the heavenly Jerusalem Edith, and thou leavest thy father in sadness, O daughter." Then he urged the deacon to keep silent about what he had said. After the service, he told Edith to prepare to go to meet Christ with her lamp burning with oil and without looking at any worldly things; for Christ was calling her, and she was soon to leave this world. At length, having given her his blessing, he left; and the appointed day drew near.

Then, on the third day after the Feast of the Exaltation of the Cross, after receiving the Body and

Blood of Christ from the hands of St. Dunstan, the holy Edith commended her soul into the hands of the Lord. She reposed in the church of St. Dionysius. Meanwhile, a certain sister ran into the main monastery from the church saying that she had heard what seemed to be a great multitude chanting psalms. And as she was listening, someone with a beautiful face and shining clothes came up to her and said: "Don't come closer, for the holy angels are about to take the girl Goda [a version of Edith's Saxon name, 'Ead-gythe'] to the eternal joys, so that, accompanied by this melody of the heavenly hosts, she may enter into the courts of eternal joy." Thus in the twenty-third year of her life, on September 16, 984, St. Edith went to Christ. And St. Dunstan buried her in the church of St. Dionysius, which she had herself constructed, and of which she had said after one visit: "This is the place of my rest, weeping all the while. Thousands of paupers were fed, and everywhere funeral Liturgies were celebrated at the request of her mother. Moreover, she built a guest-house in the yard of the monastery where twelve paupers were fed daily, a custom instituted by Edith herself.

On the thirtieth day after her repose, the saint appeared to her mother, radiant and joyful, and said that she had been accepted by her King into everlasting glory. "Satan accused me in the presence of my Lord," she said, "but by the prayers of the holy apostles I crushed his head, and by the Cross of the Lord Jesus I overthrew him and trampled on him." On that same thirtieth day there was born a little girl, whose parents had asked Edith before her death to receive her from the holy font. She said: "I shall receive her in the manner that is pleasing to God." But since Edith was born into the heavenly world before this girl into the earthly, she was brought into the church without a sponsor, and was baptized by St. Alphege, St. Ethelwold's successor in the see of Winchester. Then, in accordance with the custom of the Church, he gave her a candle, saying: "Receive this light, with which you will enter into the marriage of the Lord." Suddenly, as if Edith was holding her little hand, she took the candle and held it. The man of God understood this to be a prophecy of her election by God, and immediately asked the parents: "Bring this girl up as one who is to be betrothed to God alone, and after she has been weaned bring her to the monastery." This girl was called Brihtgiva, and later became abbess of St. Edith's monastery at Wilton, reposing in holiness in 1065.

Then St. Edith began to show by signs and wonders that she was a citizen of the heavens and was accessible to the prayers of supplicants. Now her tomb was covered with a shining white pall. One day, a woman who had been left alone there took a small part of this pall, and, wrapping it round her shin-bone, stole away. But then a Divine shackle fettered the fugitive and fixed her leg to the ground so that she could not cross the threshold with her loot. She struggled for a long time in this condition until the sacristan came and ordered her to leave. But the guilty woman remained rooted to the spot, deathly white, trembling and groaning. Then, however, she took the pall from her leg and handed it back, saying: "This bound me." Immediately she was able to walk again and left. Many witnessed this miracle and praised God; and Edith's mother was comforted in her distress.

Three years after her repose, St. Edith appeared to St. Dunstan and said: "The Lord in remembrance of His mercies has taken me up, and it has pleased His ineffable goodness that for the salvation of the faithful I should be honoured among men on earth in the same way that He has caused me to be honoured among the angels in heaven. So go to Wilton in obedience to the Divine command, and take up my body from the earth. Doubt not, and do not think that you are being deluded by some phantom; for this will be a sign of the truth of my words: except for those members of my body which I abused through childish levity, such as my eyes, hands and feet, you will find the rest of my body incorrupt. For I never knew lust or gluttony. And the thumb of my right hand, with which I used to make the sign of the Cross assiduously, you will find also incorrupt, so that the mercy of the Lord may appear in the part that has been preserved, and His Fatherly correction in the part that has been consumed." Dunstan set off for Wilton, and when he was spending the night at Sarum nearby, he was taken in a vision to the tomb of the holy virgin, where lo! he clearly saw St. Dionysius standing at the altar together with the virgin Edith, resplendent in dazzling light. She then said to Dionysius: "Thou knowest, O father, what is pleasing to God in regard to me. Therefore, as the interpreter of the Divine counsel, and legate of the Divine will, tell this man who has come by what faith and authority I have invited him here." St. Dionysius said: "Give heed, brother, to the vision thou hast just seen. What this beloved lady has just said is true. For she who deserved to be crowned among the citizens of heaven is worthy of the veneration of those on earth. Worthy of honour is this body, this temple of virginal chastity, in which the Lord and King of glory, the Lover of chastity, reigned. Such veneration which is pleasing to Christ is necessary for mortals." Therefore the holy body was raised from the earth on November 3, 987, and everything was found as had been foretold.

Once a certain Glastonbury monk named Edulph was cutting away from the holy body a piece of cloth which had been carelessly wrinkled. At the same time he struck the holy body with his scissors. Immediately blood gushed out as if from a cut vein, and poured onto the clothes and pavement. The rash brother was terrified, and, abandoning the scissors as well as the holy body, he fell on his face confessing his crime and weeping tears of repentance. When he rose the blood had completely disappeared.

Again, a sister was trying to cut away a part of the ribbon which was on the holy head. But she was prevented from doing this in a wonderful way. For the head raised itself as if alive and gave her a threatening look.

Some clerics from Brittany came to Wilton bearing with them the relics of St. Iwi, the hierodeacon and disciple of St. Cuthbert, who had spent his last years in Brittany. They placed them with honour on the monastery's altar. But when they wanted to leave, the holy relics stuck to the altar and could not be moved by any means. The foreigners wept, cried, rent their clothes, tore their hair, but to no avail. At length, Abbess Wulfrida consoled them with a gift of 2000 solidi, and they went sadly home.

A certain man who had usurped a piece of land belonging to St. Edith was apparently taken by sudden death without repentance. A little later he sat up in his coffin and said: "Help me, my friends, help me, all you God's faithful. Behold the intolerable wrath of St. Edith prevents this unhappy soul of mine from entering any part of heaven or earth. Nowhere does she allow the invader of her property to abide, neither to remain in this body nor to die." But when the land he had stolen was restored, he immediately breathed out his spirit.

Once King Canute was at Wilton for the feast of Pentecost. As he was eating, he kept laughing, declaring that he did not believe that Edith was a saint in view of the lustful habits of her father. Archbishop Ethelnoth contradicted him, and immediately opened the tomb of the virgin. And she, sitting up in the coffin, was seen to attack the abusive king. Then he, petrified, fell to the earth as if dead. At length, recovering his breath, he blushed and asked forgiveness for his rudeness; and from that moment he held the saint in great honour.

Once the same king was in trouble at sea. When he called on the name of St. Edith, the storm was suddenly stilled and he arrived safely at his chosen port. A similar miracle happened to Archbishop Aldred of York when he was sailing in the Adriatic Sea. Having called upon her name, she appeared to him visibly and said: "I am Edith". Immediately the sea became calm. [47]

ST. OSWALD
OF YORK
(February 29)

OUR holy father Oswald was the son of Danish convert parents, and was the nephew of St. Oda of Canterbury. After a certain time spent in a monastery in Winchester, he went for five or six years to the Benedictine monastery of Fleury-on-Loire. There he acquired a thorough knowledge of Benedictine monasticism and the writings of the Fathers, distinguishing himself by his humility, obedience and the austerity of his life.

In 958, when St. Oda was dying, he called his nephew, who was now a priest, to his bedside. But when Oswald arrived at Dover, he heard that the saint had already reposed. He decided not to return to Fleury, however, but to go on north to York, where another relative of his, Oscetel, was archbishop. Oscetel introduced him to St. Dunstan, and he, much impressed, introduced him to the king. And so, supported by both king and primate, he was elected to the bishopric of Worcester, where he soon became the object of great love and veneration by the citizens. [48]

Duckett writes: "The Cathedral at Worcester was dedicated to Saint Peter. Since it was very small, it soon could not hold the people who came flocking to hear this new pastor preach. Outside it, on a side, level tract of ground, stood a little stone shrine, with a cross on top, marking the burial-place of Wifred and his wife Alta, benefactors of Saint Peter's. To this open space Oswald moved his congregation and taught as best he could, standing beside the old tomb. Soon the crowds compelled the building of a new and larger church; and when at last this was ready, the bishop consecrated it in honour of Mary, Mother of God. Then the little Saint Peter's, which before Oswald's coming had seen secular clergy in its choir, offered its services in union with this more splendid cathedral." [49]

Meanwhile, in 962, Oswald had founded his first monastery, at Westbury-on-Trim, establishing in it, and later in Worcester, the regular Benedictine discipline. Then, as we have seen, he founded or re-founded several monasteries in the Severn valley, placing his own disciples in the abbacies. But his most famous foundation was outside his diocese, deep in the fen-country of Huntingdonshire - Ramsey. Here, in 971, he introduced monks from Westbury and the famous scholar Abbo of Fleury (who wrote the life of St. Edmund), and translated the relics of St. Felix of Dunwich and the holy Martyr-Princes Ethelbert and Ethelbricht of Kent. The land was donated by the pious alderman of East Anglia, Ethelwine.

Once both Oswald and Ethelwine came to a feast at the monastery. "There is an ancient tradition," writes Oswald's biographer, an anonymous monk of Ramsey, "that the whole of the main body of the congregation process barefoot to the church of the Blessed Ever-Virgin Birth-giver of God Mary, which custom was followed by the chief man [Ethelwine] as he walked with us with joyful heart together with his soldiers, the monks and the boys. But next to the church to which we had to go was a bridge, which we crossed on the way out. So on the way back we wanted to go quickly home by sailing across in a boat together with the precious relics. When the Liturgy was over, the prelate blessed the people; and we hastened to return home. But the boat was overloaded. When we were in the middle of the deep lake, and were about to sink, and the prelate was standing on the bank surrounded by his own people, he heard the sound of voices: 'Saint Benedict, help us!' On hearing this, he asked the reason, and on ascertaining it he raised his holy right hand and said, trusting in the Lord: 'May the blessing of Christ come upon us from above.' His clear voice came to the ears of the most merciful Redeemer more speedily than you could have finished the verse; and all were brought safely to land."[50]

York Minster: Church of the Mother of God

In 972, the saint was made archbishop of York while retaining the bishopric of Worcester. This appointment gave him a vast sphere of influence, but also great responsibilities and difficulties. Since the Viking invasions of the previous centuries, when the North had been to a large extent repopulated by Danes and consequently repaganized, its loyalty to the English crown had been in question. Thus Kings Edmund and Edred had had to deal with uprisings of the Northumbrians, who first took Eric Bloodaxe, son of Harold Fairhair of Norway, as their king; the Olaf Cuaran, another Viking; and then Eric again. Finally, in 954, Edred regained permanent control of the North. Archbishop Wulfstan of York, who had sided with the rebels in both Edmund's and Edred's reigns, was imprisoned, and then, perhaps on St. Dunstan's advice, was brought south and given the diocese of Dorchester, while the Danish bishop of Dorchester, Oscetel, was given York.[51] This was a bold move, but it worked — the Dane was better able than the Englishman to control his countrymen, and he was thoroughly loyal to the English crown. Indeed, both archbishops (Oda of Canterbury and Oscetel of York) were Danish at this time; and it says much for the wisdom, charity and lack of prejudice of the English leaders at this time that they were able to welcome such a situation when the Danish wars had by no means receded from the people's memory.

Since St. Oswald was of Danish parents, and, moreover, related to Oscetel, he was well equipped to continue in this tradition of racial reconciliation and missionary activity. However, the fact that he did not found a single monastery in his northern diocese shows the difficulty of the task he faced; and during the anti-monastic reaction of the next reign this diocese suffered as much as any. Thus in a memorandum on the estates of York, he states: "I, Archbishop Oswald, declare that all these lands which Archbishop Oscetel obtained in Northumbria, and which my lord granted me for St. Peter's when he was at Nottingham, together with these other lands which are entered here besides, I had them all until [?] ascended. Then St. Peter was robbed of them. May God avenge it as He will." [52]

Once when the saint was making a tour of the monasteries in his diocese, a messenger came to him from Ely announcing the death of a brother who had fallen from the walls of the church. He was saddened by this news, and asked the brethren of the monastery of Ramsey to celebrate thirty Liturgies and vigils for the dead man; which they did. He himself, meanwhile, returned to York, where he remained steadfast in prayer. One night Huna (for that was the dead man's name) appeared to him, and Oswald, seeing him stand opposite, said: "Who are you?" To which he replied: "I am he for whom you have been pouring out prayer to the Lord. I thank your paternity. Yesterday my soul was taken up to the refreshment of eternal salvation." In view of this appearance, Oswald ordered his clergy to celebrate the Divine Liturgy at daybreak. "When he came to us again," records his biographer, "he told us this story, saying: 'The Lord has heard your prayers; now the soul of the brother has been freed from punishment.' But we understand this to have happened through his prayers, for we have learned from the Scriptures that the prayers of a righteous man avail much."[53]

On another occasion, the saint entered a hall in York after celebrating the Divine Liturgy. "Having commanded blessed water to be sprinkled through the house, he sat down and prepared to eat the good things of his Lord, blessing Him in His works. There is an ancient custom among the English that the people go up to the bishop or priest and, holding their hands in the shape of the Cross, receive some blessed bread from him before returning to their seats and eating their food.[54] And when he had given a piece to everyone, and they had reverently returned to their seats and were eating with gratitude, the father placed a piece of bread next to his seat. And he was happy, because the hall was full. Meanwhile, while they were all eating their bread, a wretched mouse, greedy in heart and mouth, boldly ate a crumb of blessed bread. But while he had the power to touch it, he could not swallow it. For that which is the guard of Christians was his downfall. After a while, some notables from the city came in bearing gifts for the lovable man. As was the custom, he received them with thanks. But they asked him to give them some blessed bread. He stretched out his hand to take that which he had placed nearby. But then he saw the wretched mouse lying there dead. Neither knowing nor caring why this had taken place, he ordered the dead mouse to be thrown out. But his servers were not slow to point out why this happened." [55]

The saint performed many miracles during his life on earth. Thus once he drove away a demon that was preventing the removal of a large stone, and on another occasion he healed a sick man with blessed bread. Again, a terrified server once saw an angel serving with him at the Divine Liturgy.

In 991 the saint visited Ramsey for the last time, to reopen the church which had been damaged by the fall of the tower. Two days later, announcing that his death was approaching, he made his last farewells to the monks. Then he returned to Worcester, where he spent the winter. [56]

After morning prayers on February 29, 992, St. Oswald came, as was his custom during Lent, to wash the feet of twelve poor men, chanting in the meantime the fifteen psalms of degrees. At the end of the psalms, the brethren bent their knees, saying, 'The Lord bless thee out of Sion, He that made heaven and the earth.' "Then blessed Oswald," continues his biographer, "also bent the knee with them before the feet of the Lord, and as he was saying 'Glory be to the Father and to the Son and the Holy Spirit', by the secret command of God his holy spirit left his body and was taken up to the heights of the eternal Kingdom... Then the brethren washed the beloved body of Oswald and clothed it in new vestments for the funeral... But since the death of such a great father could not be kept hidden, lamentation quickly spread through the houses, castles and countryside. And merchants left their markets, women their looms, hurrying to the door of the man of God. Orphans and widows, strangers, peasants, monks and clergy, all groaned with great sorrow and wept." [57]

Many miracles took place at the tomb of the saint; and in response to these and a special heavenly revelation, Archbishop Erdulf of York translated the holy body on April 15, 1004. A great multitude was present at the translation, one of whom, a woman with a paralysed hand, was healed of her infirmity. However, there was also an abbot there who by his words and gestures tried to cast doubt on the whole proceedings. This saddened the bishops and other good men, and they turned to Christ in prayer that the doubter should be convinced and St. Oswald glorified. While they were praying a sufferer was brought into their midst who was lame and covered all over with leprosy. He was placed beside the body of the saint. After prayers he was found completely healed. Seeing this, the crowd rejoiced and praised God, while the former doubters prostrated themselves in tears to the ground, asking forgiveness for their sin. The bones of the saint were then washed and placed in a reliquary at Worcester. Many healings were wrought through the water used in the washing: the blind saw, the deaf heard, and the infirm were restored to full strength. All the clothes of the saint had been reduced to dust except his chasuble, which was completely untouched by corruption.

At the monastery of Ramsey, there was a very pious monk name Edwaker, who had a cancerous ulcer on his jaw. This became so bad and disgusting to behold that, in obedience to the abbot and his brethren, he betook himself to a small island near the monastery, where food was brought to him and his attendant every day. On St. Oswald's day he came to the monastery with his attendant and stood listening to the prayers in a hidden corner of the church. After the service, the brethren, taking pity on him, persuaded him to come with them to the refectory, although he was all for going back to his island. Now there was a custom in the monastery on that day to pass round the goblet which St. Oswald had drunk from during his earthly life. Every brother drank from it and received a blessing thereby. Last of all it came to the sick brother. Recognizing the cup as St. Oswald's, he groaned and lifted up his voice and mind in prayer to God to heal him through the intercession of the saint. The eyes of all those sitting round were fastened on him, and the hearts of all joined in his prayer. Having asked a blessing from those around him, he drank. Immediately his ulcer disappeared, and for the rest of his life that side of his face was a little rosier than the other.

There was a citizen of Worcester who had been dumb from his birth, and who had the habit of going to church and standing in the place where the clergy passed most often, bending his head to show the humble respect which his mouth was not able to utter. One feastday, he came to the church and was standing in his usual place when he saw someone whom he did not know coming to him from the tomb of St. Oswald. This man had a venerable face and shining white hair, was dressed in priestly vestments and was holding a staff in his hand. He came to the dumb man as he was inclining his head and struck him on the neck. Then he disappeared. At this blow a great mass of coagulated blood fell out of the man's mouth and onto the floor. "Help, help," he cried, "throw me out quickly, in case the church of the Lord is defiled by my blood." So he was led out by those standing near, who were amazed at the very plentiful flow of blood. While he was washing he explained to them what had happened; and hearing the formerly dumb man speak, they were very ready to believe him.

Once Worcester was on fire through the negligence of its citizens. The monks brought the shrine of St. Oswald out of the church, meaning to take it to the part of the city where the fire was fiercest. But suddenly the light shrine became unbearably heavy. So they changed their route and came to the house of a poor man who was standing outside it sadly waiting for its complete destruction. On seeing the fathers, however, he cheered up and besought them to take the shrine through the burning house. This they did; and immediately the flames died out.

On another occasion, the city was again on fire, and the shrine of St. Oswald was carried to the burning part. A certain man who had just built a big house asked the monks to carry the saint's shrine into his house, saying: "Holy Father and Hierarch Oswald, look! I give you my house which is in danger from the flames. I place it under your dominion by perpetual right! Vindicate me, free me from this present danger." Having said this, he ordered the shingles on the roof of his house to be thrown down. His order was obeyed, but live coals fell like hail on those who were carrying out his command on the roof of the house. Nevertheless, it was preserved completely unharmed at the intercession of St. Oswald. An adjacent house, however, was completely burned down except for one log. The shingles, too, were consumed.

Again, a pestilence was raging through Worcester and the neighbouring villages. A healthy man would be walking or sitting outside his home when he would suddenly fall and die without confession or communion. The brethren of the church of the Mother of God then brought the shrine of the saint in a procession round the city, singing a litany meanwhile. Immediately the pestilence ceased, not only in Worcester, but also in the neighbouring villages whose inhabitants had come to take part in the litany and procession. But those who had disdained to take part were struck down. The monks of Pershore were also hit by the disease. One of them asked his brother according to the flesh, a monk from Worcester, to take him to St. Oswald. A carriage was prepared, he was carried to the saint's shrine, and within a few days he was completely cured. But those who remained in the monastery soon died. [58]

APPENDIX

NOTES ON THE MONASTERIES

The monastic revival began when St. Dunstan became abbot of Glastonbury in 943. Glastonbury was the most famous and ancient centre, not only of monasticism, but of Christianity generally, in the whole of the British Isles. Founded, according to tradition, by St. Joseph of Arimathea, it was refounded by King Lucius late in the second century, and became a centre of Celtic monasticism associated with such illustrious saints as Patrick, David and Gildas the Wise. Nor did it cease to be a monastic centre when the Saxons came: King Ine of Wessex in the seventh century, and St. Dunstan in the tenth, both gave a strong impetus to its spiritual life. King Edgar placed it directly under the jurisdiction of the Pope so as to ensure that no local landlord gained control over it. [59]

Other monasteries in the west of England included Athelney, which had been founded by King Alfred.[60] Bath was one of the monasteries which St. Dunstan supervised, and for a time it (together with Deerhurst) was ruled by another of the great figures of English Orthodoxy — St. Alphege, the future hieromartyr archbishop of Canterbury. Tavistock was founded by Alderman Ordulph of Devon and Cornwall in 981, and it was he who obtained the relics of St. Rumon for it from the Celtic monastery of Ruan Lanihorne. [61]

Malmesbury was founded by the Irishman Maeldub in the seventh century, and was made famous by Maeldub's disciple, St. Aldhelm, who was buried there by St. Egwin in 709. St. Dunstan restored the monastery, and in 986, after prophesying the imminent invasion of the Danes, he transferred the relics of St. Aldhelm from the bejewelled shrine which King Athelstan had made for them to a plain stone tomb to the right of the altar. After his death, and in accordance with his prophecy, the Danes came and broke into the monastery. One was about to cut off the gems from the saint's shrine when he was thrown to the ground as if stabbed. The rest fled, struck with terror. [62]

Of the Severn valley monasteries, the oldest was Evesham, which was founded by St. Egwin in the seventh century on the site of an appearance of the Mother of God. St. Egwin, like his friend St. Aldhelm, is known to have acted in defence of his monastery's rights long after his repose.

Winchcombe was a ninth-century foundation glorified by the relics of the Martyr-King Kenelm of Mercia. [63] It was restored by St. Oswald, bishop of Worcester, who placed his companion in asceticism, Germanus, as abbot there. He also placed Germanus in charge of the new foundation at Westbury-on-Trim. And at Pershore he installed an abbot named Fordbricht, who had been trained under St. Dunstan at Glastonbury and St. Ethelwold at Abingdon. Pershore was enriched by some relics of St. Edburga, and was henceforward dedicated to SS. Mary, Peter and Paul, and Edburga. [64]

The other main group of monasteries was in the fen-country of East Anglia. This had been a great centre of monasticism already in the seventh century, when there lived such great saints as Felix at Soham, Fursey at Burgh Castle, Etheldreda and her sisters at Ely, Botulph at Ikanhoe and Guthlac at Croyland. However, the ravages of the Danes in the late ninth century had left the area a wasteland — until King Edgar determined to restore it to its former glory. Working together with St. Ethelwold, he refounded Ely, Peterborough, Thorney and other smaller monasteries. Land was bought and cleared, abbots of stricter discipline imported, and the veneration of forgotten local saints revived.

Hand of St. Etheldreda. *Courtesy of the Vicar, Roman Catholic Church of St. Etheldreda, Ely.*

Eleanor Duckett has described the re-founding of Thorney thus: "This 'Isle of Thorns' in the midst of the waters of the great marsh had once been, it was said, the home of three hermits, Tancred and Torhtred, and their sister, Tova, who settled to her prayer a little distance from them, in the heart of the thickets. They were following, we may think, in the line of a few adventurers in religion who had come in the seventh century from Medeshamstede [Peterborough], having gained permission from their abbot, Saxulf, to retreat into this deeper solitude. In the time of these brothers and their sister the Danes arrived to destroy. The tradition of Aethelwold [Ethelwold] relates that he bought the ruins the Danes had left from their owner, Aethelflaed [Ethelfleda], that he installed some monks — the number is given as twelve — and built for them in 972-3 an abbey with its church, dedicating the altar at the east end to Our Lady, the west end to Saint Peter, and a chapel in the north transept to Saint Benedict. This account points to an altar at either end, after Carolingian custom.

To Ely, which Edgar and Ethelwold refounded as a monastery for men, another Abingdon monk, Brihtnoth, was brought as abbot. Ely was the home of the incorrupt body of St. Etheldreda.

Not content with having the relics of St. Etheldreda and her holy sisters Sexburga and Ermenhilda, Brihtnoth also desired the relics of the fourth sister, the hermitess St. Withburga. So, after fasting and prayer, he and some of his monks travelled to the little monastery of East Dereham in Norfolk, where St. Withburga had struggled. Then he carried off the holy relics, to the displeasure of the monks and citizens of Dereham.

Some years later, during the reign of King Ethelred and the abbacy of Aelsi, the fifth of the holy daughters of King Anna, the hermitess Wendreda, was translated from March to Ely, where it was enclosed in a shrine of gold adorned with precious stones. [65]

Again, when a little monastery was founded at Eynesbury, relics were found to be wanting. So a conspiracy was formed with the warden of St. Neot's shrine at Neotstoke, Cornwall. On November 30, 974, he stole the body of the saint, and arrived with it at Eynesbury (later renamed St. Neot's) on December 7. But the Cornishmen soon discovered the theft and traced the body to Eynesbury. So angry were they that King Edgar was forced to send out an armed force to drive the Cornishmen out of the village. [66]

One may wonder whether the forced translations were in accordance with the will of God. However, holy relics were held to be an essential possession of any newly founded monastery; so where they could not be freely obtained, it was held to be no sin to take them by stealth, as Rachel stole her father's gods (Gen. 31.31-35). In any case, the practice continued, as can be seen from the forcible translation of St. Mildred's relics from Minster-in-Thanet to Canterbury in the reign of King Canute. [67]

NOTES

(1) Epistle 33; quoted in Abbé Guettée, *The Papacy*, New York, Minos, 1966, and The Orthodox Christian Witness, August 3/16, 1981.

(2) *The History of the Norman Conquest*, Vol. I, p. 1.

(3) *The Normans and Their Myth*, London, Thames & Hudson, 1976, p. 103.

(4) Quoted in Abbé Guettée, op. cit, p. 305, note.

(5) See John Meyendorff, "Rome and Orthodoxy: Authority or Truth?" in P. J. McCord (ed.), *A Pope for All Christians*, London: SPCK, 1977, p. 135.

(6) See A. W. Haddan & W. Stubbs, *Councils and Ecclesiastical Documents Relating to Great Britain and Ireland*, Oxford: The Clarendon Press, 1871, Vol. III, pp. 650, 655, 658-9. The homily is translated in Henry Soames, *An Inquiry into the Doctrine of the Anglo-Saxon Church*, Oxford, 1930, pp. 349-52. See also V. Moss, "Western Saints and the Filioque," *Living Orthodoxy*, February 1981.

(7) Quoted in Richard Haugh, *Photius and the Carolingians*, Belmont, MA: Nordland, 1975, pp. 129-30.

(8) See Walter Ullmann, *Medieval Political Thought*, Harmondsworth: Penguin Books, 1970, p. 93

(9) Saxon Priest B., "Vita Dunstani," in W. Stubbs, *Memorials of St. Dunstan*, Rolls series, 1874. The rest of this account is taken from the other early (11th c.)

lives of St. Dunstan by Abelard, Osbert and Edmer, in Stubbs, op. cit.; William Malmesbury, *Gesta Regum Anglorum* and *Gesta Pontificum Anglorum*; and Eleanor Duckett, *Saint Dunstan of Canterbury*, London: Collins, 1955.

(10) According to William of Malmesbury (*De Antiquitate Glastoniae Ecclesiae*, 2) a 10th c. Glastonbury calendar and an 11th c. scholiast on Fiacc's hymn, St. Patrick returned to Britain after his apostolate in Ireland and may even have been buried at Glastonbury.

(11) Adelard ("Vita Dunstani," in Stubbs, op. cit., p. 58) states that Edred was buried in the Old Minster. However, Farmer (*The Oxford Dictionary of Saints*, Oxford: The Clarendon Press, 1978, p. 112) says that he was buried in Glastonbury.

(12) *Gesta Regum Anglorum*, II, p. 8; Adelard, "Vita Dunstani, in Stubbs, op. cit., p. 56

(13) See Christopher Brook, *The Saxon and Norman Kings*, Fontana, 1963, pp. 127-8.

(14) See the references in note 9.

(15) William of Malmesbury, *Gesta Pontificum Anglorum*, I, 14.

(16) Anonymous, "Vita Oswaldi, in J. Raine, *Historians of the Church of York*, Rolls series, 1874, vol. I, pp. 406-7.

(17) Saxon Priest B., ita Dunstani, in W. Stubbs, *Memorials of St. Dunstan*, op. cit.

(18) William of Malmesbury, *Gesta Pontificum Anglorum*, I, 14.

(19) *Lives of the Saints*, Early English Texts Society, no. 76, 1881.

(20) Ibid.

(21) "Passio et Miracula Sancti Edwardi Regis et Martyris." Text in Christine Fell, *Edward King and Martyr,* University of Leeds, 1971. Unless otherwise indicated, this, together with *The Anglo-Saxon Chronicle,* is the main source used in this account.

(22) *Anglo-Saxon Chronicle,* D, 975.

(23) Anonymous, "History of St. Cuthbert"; translated by Dorothy Whitelock, *English Historical Documents,* London: Eyre & Spottiswood, 1955, pp. 838-40.

(24) See D. J. V. Fisher, "The Anti-Monastic Reaction in the Reign of Edward the Martyr," Cambridge Historical Journal, 1952, X, pp. 254-70.

(25) According to the *Vita Oswaldi,* it was certain "zealous thegns" of Edward's who were responsible for his murder, preferring Ethelred "because he appeared to be gentler in speech and words" than his brother. However, Theodoric Paulis (quoted in Orthodoxy America, May-June, 1981) wrote that "St. Edward was a young man of great dvotion and excellent conduct; he was wholly Catholic, good and of holy life; moreover, above all things he loved God and the Church; he was generous to the poor, a haven to the good, a champion of the Faith of Christ, a vessel full of every virtuous grace."

(26) *Gesta Pontificum Anglorum,* II, 9.

(27) *Gesta Regum Anglorum,* 161.

(28) J. M. Kemble, *Codex Diplomaticus Aevi Saxoni,* 1845-8, no. 706.

(29) J. Wilson-Claridge, *The Recorded Miracles of St. Edward the Martyr,* Brookwood: King Edward Orthodox Trust, 1984.

(30) *Vita Ethelwoldi*, translated in Whitelock, op. cit., p. 840.

(31) Ibid., chapter 24.

(32) Denis Brearley and Marianne Goodfellow, "Wulfstan's Life of Saint Ethelwold: A Translation with Notes," Revue de l'Universite d'Ottawa/University of Ottawa Quarterly, vol. 52, no.3, pp. 397-407.

(33) *Vita Ethelwoldi.*

(34) Ibid.

(35) Ibid.

(36) Osbert, "Vita Dunstani"; Stubbs, op. cit., p. 113.

(37) *Saint Dunstan of Canterbury*, op. cit., pp. 95-6.

(38) Op. cit., p. 141.

(39) Duckett, op. cit., p. 221.

(40) "Vita Ethelwoldi."

(41) Ibid.

(42) Brearley & Goodfellow, op. cit.

(43) Ibid.

(44) Ibid.

(45) Ibid.

(46) Until the 13th century, in the West, as in the Orthodox Church to this day, the sign of the Cross was made with the thumb and two fingers. See *Dictionnaire de l'Archeologie Chretienne*, tome III, c. 3143.

(47) This account is taken from Goscelin's lives of the saint in Migne, *Patrologia Latina*, Paris, 1850, vol. 155, 111-116, and A. Wilmart, "La Legende de Ste. Edith en Prose et Vers par le Moine Goscelin," *Analecta Bollandiana*, 1938, LVI, 5-101, 265-307.

(48) This account is drawn mainly from anonymous, "Vita Oswaldi," Raine, op. cit., pp. 410-21.

(49) Op. cit., pp. 140-1.

(50) Edmer, "Vita Oswaldi," in Raine, op. cit., vol. II, pp. 28-9.

(51) We know that St. Dunstan venerated the relics of St. Cuthbert at Chester-le-Street sometine during the reign of King Edred. It is possible that he was on a mission to bring Archbishop Wulfstan south with him. In this account of Archbishop Wulfstan, I follow Hunt (*The English Church*, p. 341). But Stenton (*Anglo-Saxon England*, p. 361, note 1) quotes a source indicating that Wulfstan was restored to his archbishopric before Edred's death.

(52) Whitelock, op. cit., pp. 521-22.

(53) "Vita Oswaldi"; in Raine, op. cit., pp. 453-4.

(54) Another custom that can be observed in the Orthodox Church today, at the end of the Divine Liturgy.

(55) "Vita Oswaldi"; in Raine, op. cit., pp. 454-5.

(56) Farmer, op. cit., p. 306.

(57) "Vita Oswaldi"; in Raine, op. cit., pp. 471-2.

(58) Edmer, "Miracula Sancti Oswaldi Archiepiscopi"; in Raine, op. cit., vol. II, pp. 11-12, 23-4, 32, 26.

(59) That such a measure was necessary is demonstrated by the letter of Pope John XII to Alderman Alfric in the riegn of King Ethelred, translated in Whitelock, op. cit., p. 824.

(60) See above, chapter 20.

(61) Farmer, op. cit., p. 350

(62) *Gesta Pontificum Anglorum, V, pp. 255-6.*

(63) W. D. Macray, *Chronicon Abbatiae de Evesham,* Rolls series, chapter 7.

(64) Farmer, op. cit., p. 118.

(65) *Liber Eliensis, 76, 77.*

(66) "Vita S. Neoti," in Whitaker, *The Life of St. Neot*, 1809.

(67) Dom Gregory Bish, *Minster Abbey 670 to 1965.*

INDEX

OTHER PUBLICATIONS FROM

ST. NECTARIOS PRESS

LIVES OF SAINTS

(A small selection)

SAINTS OF ANGLE-SAXON ENGLAND, VOLUME 1

by Vladimir Moss

The first volume of this present series of little-known saints from 9th to 11th century England. It contains accounts of 19 saints from 780 to the mid 900's. 100pp. Illus. Paper
$8.50 + shipping

SAINTS OF ENGLAND'S GOLDEN AGE

by Vladimir Moss

The lives of almost fifty saints of England from the seventh and early eighth centuries, most of which are not well-known and are presented here in modern English translation for the first time. FORTHCOMING IN 1994

SUFFERING OF THE GREAT MARTYR CATHERINE

Translated from the Greek by Lizardos and Papadopulos. A favorite for Orthodox, this life is illustrated with an icon of the saint and many photographs of the monastery dedicated to her in Sinai. 32pp. illus. Paper $2.00 + shipping

THE PASSION AND MIRACLES OF THE GREAT MARTYR SAINT GEORGE

The life of this favorite saint of East and West in a handsome edition printed on acid-free paper, with many icons illustrating his life and martyrdom. 50pp. Paper $4.00 + shipping

SHIPPING: 12% (Min. $2.00)

OTHER TITLES

A LENTEN COOKBOOK FOR ORTHODOX CHRISTIANS

Our first lenten cookbook containing scores of Lenten recipes and a full alphabetical index. Also has the life of St. Euphrosynos the Cook and and outline of the complete Orthodox fasting rules. 260pp. Paper $8.50 + shipping

REVIEWER'S COMMENTS:

"FROM PERSONAL EXPERIENCE OVER SEVERAL LENTEN FASTS, I CAN TESTIFY TO THE EXCELLENCE OF MANY RECIPES IN A LENTEN COOKBOOK FOR ORTHODOX CHRISTIANS. *EASTERN CHURCHES REVIEW*, KALLISTOS WARE, LECTURER IN EASTERN CHURCH HISTORY, OXFORD UNIVERSITY (Presently an Orthodox Bishop in England).

THE HOLY NATIVITY OF OUR LORD: The Birth of the Messiah

by Euphemia Briere

Profusely illustrated with iconographic line drawings, this account of the Nativity of Our Saviour is a lovely book for children of various ages.

20pp. Large format Paper $6.00

SECULAR HUMANISM: An Orthodox Perspective

by Father John Bockman. A well-documented study of a contemporary neo-pagan movement which has permeated and manipulated American society to eliminate a Christian worldview. It contains an extensive bibliography.

84pp Paper $8.00 + shipping

SHIPPING: 12% (Min. $2.00)